miracles happen

JOEL OSTEEN

Miracles Happen: Your Journey to a Supernatural Breakthrough

Copyright © 2024 Joel Osteen

All rights reserved. No part of this book may be reproduced or transmitted in any form or by any means, electronic or mechanical, including photocopying, recording, or by any information storage and retrieval system, without permission in writing from the publisher.

Scripture quotations marked MSG are taken from The Message, copyright © 1993, 2002, 2018 by Eugene H. Peterson. Used by permission of NavPress. All rights reserved. Represented by Tyndale House Publishers.

Scripture quotations marked NIV are taken from the Holy Bible, New International Version®, NIV®. Copyright © 1973, 1978, 1984, 2011 by Biblica, Inc.™ Used by permission of Zondervan. All rights reserved worldwide. www.zondervan.com The "NIV" and "New International Version" are trademarks registered in the United States Patent and Trademark Office by Biblica, Inc.™

Scripture quotations marked NKJV are taken from the New King James Version®. Copyright © 1982 by Thomas Nelson. Used by permission. All rights reserved.

Scripture quotations marked NLT are taken from the Holy Bible, New Living Translation, copyright © 1996, 2004, 2015 by Tyndale House Foundation. Used by permission of Tyndale House Publishers, Carol Stream, Illinois 60188. All rights reserved.

ISBN: 978-1-963492-01-9

Created and assembled for Joel Osteen Ministries by
Breakfast for Seven
breakfastforseven.com

Printed in the United States of America.

For additional resources by Joel Osteen, visit JoelOsteen.com.

contents

Introduction vii

30 Miracles to Inspire You

1 Your Breakthrough Is Going to Happen Quickly 1
The Parting of the Red Sea

2 Your Burning Bush Is on the Way 5
The Burning Bush

3 Praise: Your Path to the Promise 9
Jericho Walls Fall

4 God's Got You 13
Daniel Delivered from the Lion's Den

5 Turning Your Mistakes into Miracles 17
Jonah and the Whale

6 In the Heat Is Your Miracle 21
Shadrach, Meshach, and Abednego

7 Your Mistakes Don't Cancel Your Destiny 25
Samson Pulls Down Temple Pillars

8 Special Strength Is Coming 29
Transfiguration of Christ

9 "Net-Breaking" Blessings 33
The Miraculous Catch of Fish

10 Roll Away Your Stone 37
Lazarus Raised from the Dead

11 God's Goodness Test 41
God Provides Manna

12 Your Favor Connection 45
Elijah Translated into Heaven

13 You Are Invisible to the Enemy 49
Syrian Army Is Blinded

14 Your Best Is Next 53
Water Turned to Wine

15 Keep on Walking 57
Healing of the Ten Lepers

16 Tapping into God's Power 61
Jesus' Resurrection

17 Let Your Faith Show 65
Paul Heals the Lame Man

18 Your Victory Begins in the Dark 69
Earthquake Frees Paul and Silas

19 Secure in His Plans for You 73
Jesus Appears to Saul

20 Your Answer Is Coming Sooner Than Expected 77
Angel Frees Peter

21 Better Together 81
Holy Spirit Descends

22 Increase Your Capacity 85
Widow's Oil

23 Your Yes Is Coming 89
Hezekiah's Healing

24 You Don't Need a Sign 93
Sundial Shadow Moves Backward

25 God Will Complete Your Incompleteness 97
Man Raised from the Dead

26 Stay Open to God's Way 101
Jesus Walks on Water

27 Your Gifts Will Return 105
Cornelius' Vision

28 Mix Your Faith 109
A Cana Man Healed

29 Stretch Out 113
A Withered Hand Is Healed

30 Your Turnaround Is Coming 117
Widow's Son Raised from the Dead

Modern-Day Miracles
Cured of Cancer 123
Mailroom Miracle 125
Securing the Compaq Center 127
Medical Missions Vision 129
Surgical Equipment Miracle 131

Miracles of the Bible
Old Testament 135
New Testament 139

Introduction

Miracles Require Faith

God is often referred to as a 'miracle-working God' because of His nature and His power. He is fundamentally good, desiring to do good things for us. Also, He is mighty, possessing all available power; He acts easily and effortlessly. Since He never changes, He is the same 'miracle-working God' today as in biblical times. We may not realize it, but miracles happen all around us.

Miracles are extraordinary events that defy natural explanation. They are God intervening in our lives as evidence that He exists, has the power, and truly cares for us. He is not bound by the laws of nature and has the power to act in ways that go beyond human understanding. Miracles reveal His glory and perfectly fulfill His will.

The Bible says, *"By faith the people passed through the Red Sea as on dry land; but when the Egyptians tried to do so, they were drowned. By faith the walls of Jericho fell, after the army had marched around them for seven days."* (Hebrews 11:29–30, NIV). These are miracles which occurred because faith was put into action.

"It's impossible to please God apart from faith. And why? Because anyone who wants to approach God must believe both that he exists and that he cares enough to respond to those who seek him" (Hebrews 11:6, MSG). Faith is an essential element for a miracle to happen. The Bible records numerous miracles — some are

detailed, others we are given little description. The Old Testament lists about eighty-three miracles, with over eighty in the New Testament.

Reading about God's miracles increases our faith in His power to intervene in our lives. While all miracles are significant, I want to highlight in this book thirty miracles to inspire and strengthen your faith. Each miracle includes a key principle to help you believe for a miracle in your life, followed by a personal exhortation.

Victoria and I desire for you to personally experience the supernatural power of God. We pray that this book will fan the flame of your faith into a roaring blaze to where you will step out in boldness to believe God for enormous miracles. Miracles happen, and we pray they will happen for you and your family, in Jesus' name.

Your Journey to a Supernatural Breakthrough

1 Your Breakthrough Is Going to Happen Quickly

The Parting of the Red Sea
Read: Exodus 14:21–24

When God brought the Israelites out of slavery, they were headed toward the Promised Land. Then Pharaoh, who had just let them go, changed his mind and decided he wanted them back. He sent six hundred of his fastest chariots and some of his strongest warriors to recapture them. The Israelites, numbering two million, found themselves at a dead end at the Red Sea. They were trapped, with nowhere to go. It seemed they would be recaptured, but at God's instructions, Moses held up his rod and the Red Sea parted, allowing the Israelites to pass through on dry ground. When Pharaoh's men came chasing them, the waters closed back up, and they were all drowned.

Psalm 114 gives us insight into what happened. Verse 3 says, *"The Red Sea saw them coming and hurried out of their way"* (NLT). That's not natural; that's supernatural. When it's your time, don't worry; enemies are going to hurry out of your way. That addiction, that debt, the anxiety — it's about to hurry out of your way. It's going to happen quickly. You may not have seen any sign of things changing; nothing looked any different, but suddenly the waters part, suddenly your health turns around, suddenly the door opens. God knows how to take things that seem permanent and change them quickly.

The Red Sea saw them coming and hurried out of their way.
Psalm 114:3 (NLT)

When God told Moses to hold up his rod and the waters would part, I'm sure Moses was tempted to reason it out. "God, what do you mean? These waters have been this way for years."

Everything in Moses' mind must have said, *It's impossible to get across. It would take months of a drought, maybe even years, and all we have is a few hours before we'll be recaptured.* But God doesn't always do things on a normal timetable. He specializes in doing a quick work. He knows how to speed things up. He caused the wind to blow back the waters, and they hurried out of the Israelites' way.

It's easy to get discouraged and accept that it's going to be this way for a long time. However, God said in Isaiah 60:22,

"I am the LORD; in its time, I will do this swiftly" (NIV). God has ordained certain moments in your life where He's going to do a quick work. It's going to happen much faster than you thought.

Instead of complaining and thinking, *This is taking so long; I don't think I'll ever get well; I'll never get out of debt, turn it around.* Say, "Father, thank You that my health is about to suddenly improve. Thank You that this addiction is not permanent and is about to quickly change and hurry out of my way." That's not just being positive; you are applying your faith in God to the situation, creating the possibility for God to speed things up. Your miracle can happen quickly.

Be Encouraged Today:

Problems that have held you back for so long are about to suddenly resolve. You're going to see a rapid turnaround, a sudden breakthrough, a speedy recovery.

2

Your Burning Bush Is on the Way

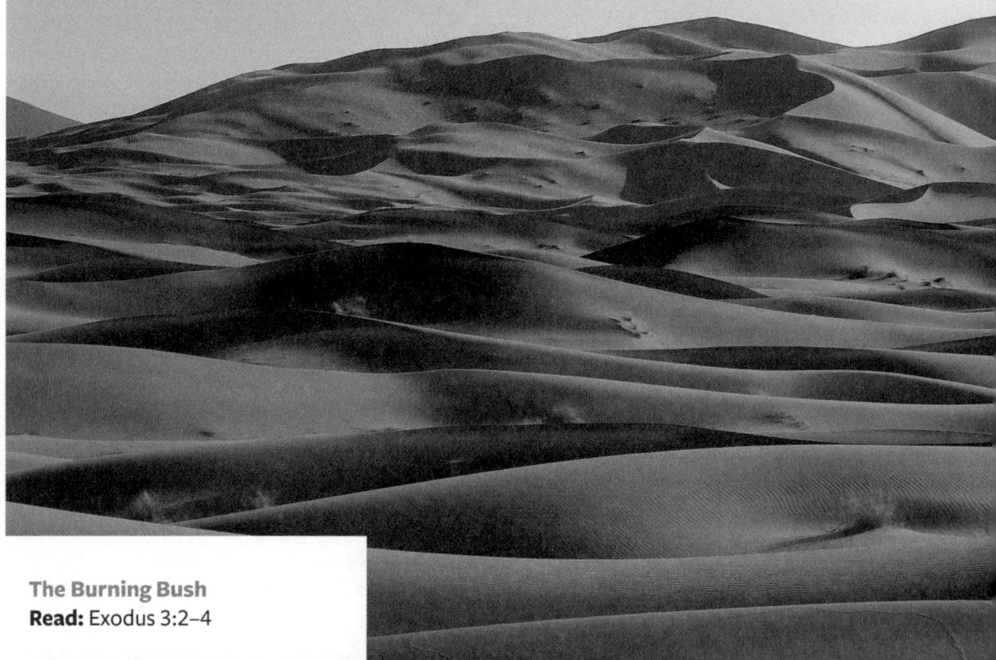

The Burning Bush
Read: Exodus 3:2–4

One morning while Moses was in the desert, a bush suddenly exploded into flames and caught fire. What made this event unique is that the bush didn't burn up. Intrigued, Moses went over to it, and a voice boomed out, "Moses, Moses, take off your sandals; you are standing on holy ground."

It had been forty years since he'd heard God's voice. A season of silence so long, he thought God had forgotten about him. He saw no future, and the purpose for his life seemed to have died. He had already accepted that he had missed his destiny. But at eighty years old, after his mistakes and all his failures, God said, "Now I'm ready for you to go deliver the Israelites." Moses, by the mighty power of God, freed a slave nation from the mightiest nation at the time and led them into their destiny.

Like Moses, you may have made mistakes and gone through setbacks, thinking you could never accomplish what's in your heart. It's been too long. But that season of silence doesn't mean God has forgotten about you. In those forty years Moses was in the desert, the scripture says he became the humblest man in all the land. In the silent years, God is still working — perhaps working on you. You may not realize it, but He's getting you prepared for a miracle.

This vision is for a future time. It describes the end, and it will be fulfilled. If it seems slow in coming, wait patiently, for it will surely take place. It will not be delayed.
Habakkuk 2:3 (NLT)

I encourage you to not go around down on yourself, thinking you've seen your best days; stir your faith up. The Lord God Almighty is at work in your life right now. What seems dead will come to life. What He promised is still going to come to pass.

Favor is coming, healing is coming, promotion is coming, freedom is coming, breakthroughs are coming, the fullness of your destiny is coming. There is a miracle ahead for you. Wait patiently and it will come to pass.

Be Encouraged Today:

Your burning bush is on the way. What God started, He's still going to bring to pass. Even if your mistakes were your fault, He's still going to bless you, He's still going to show you favor, He's still going to open doors that you couldn't open if you just stay close to Him.

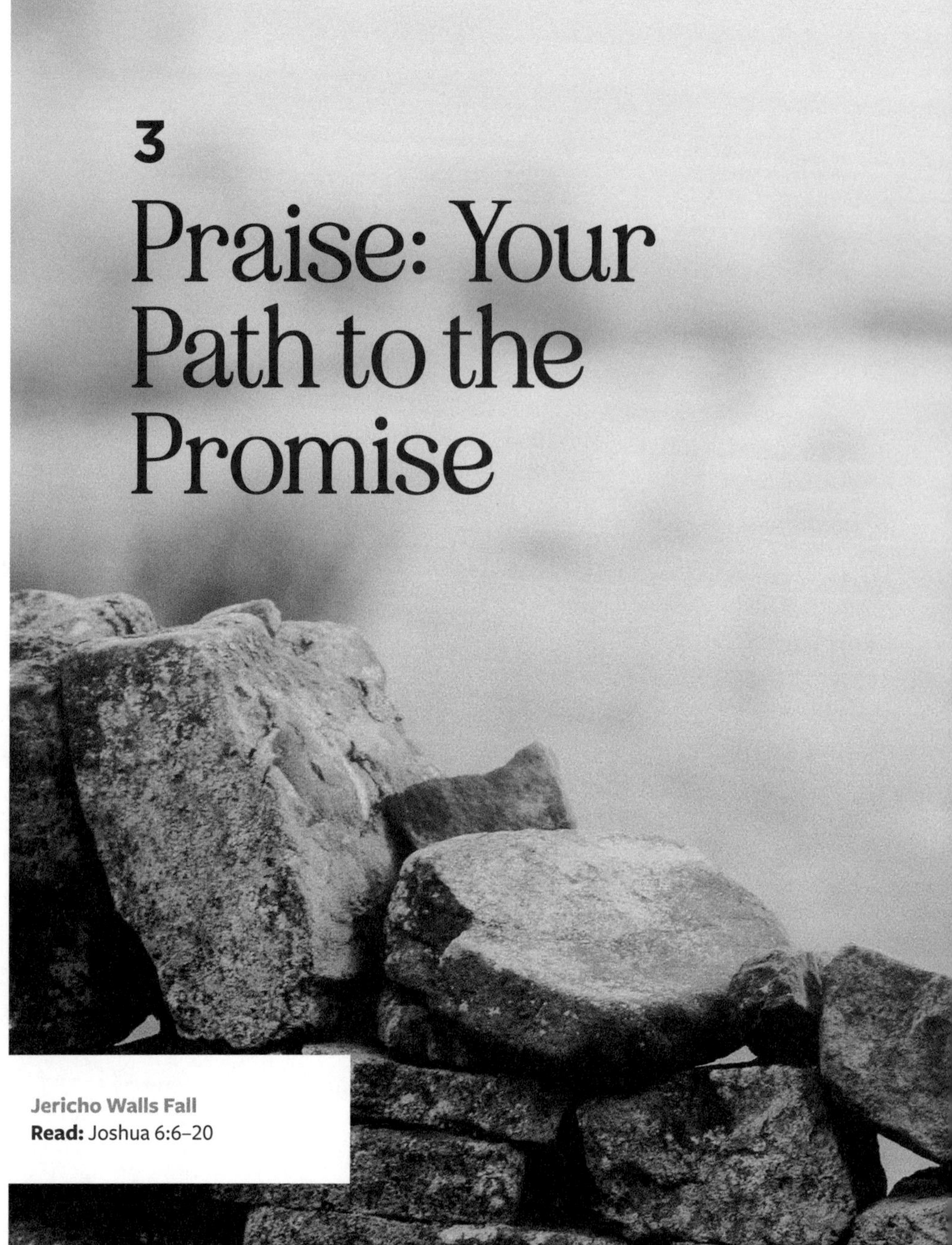

3

Praise: Your Path to the Promise

Jericho Walls Fall
Read: Joshua 6:6–20

For forty years, the Israelites traveled through the desert, aiming to reach the Promised Land. Their parents never made it because of their negative attitude and complaints. They lacked faith and eventually died. Now their children were trying to enter, and their obstacle was Jericho, the last city standing between them and the Promised Land. You can imagine how excited they were. If they could get through Jericho, they would see their dream come to pass.

There's always a "Jericho" standing between you and your Promised Land, one last obstacle that looks insurmountable. You've come this far, you're so close, but you don't see how you can get past it. That's how the Israelites felt. They were excited on one hand and discouraged on the other. After years, they were finally within reach and could taste victory, but Jericho had a

huge wall around it. It was so thick that chariots rode on top of it. To conquer Jericho seemed impossible.

I will bless the Lord at all times, His praise shall continually be in my mouth.
Psalm 34:1 (NKJV)

God told Joshua to have them march around the wall for six days, and on the seventh day, on the seventh time around, they were to let out a great shout of praise. I'm sure they thought, *Joshua, we'll shout after the walls fall, after we take the city, then we'll celebrate.* Joshua said, "No, you're missing the point. The shout is what's going to cause the wall to fall." The Bible says, *"It was by faith that the people of Israel marched around Jericho for seven days, and the walls came crashing down"* (Hebrews 11:30, NLT).

Like them, we want to shout after the victory. But God says, "If you'll praise Me while the wall is still standing, then you'll see things begin to change." Will you trust God enough to praise Him in front of a wall that's not moving, to worship Him despite a bad medical report, to thank Him for freedom when you still have the addiction?

The great shout of praise didn't make sense. "Why are you praising? You're on the outside; you'll never get past this wall." The Israelites stood in front of that wall and let out

a great shout of praise, and suddenly that huge wall came tumbling down. It crumbled in such a way as to form a ramp, so the Israelites could go in and take the city.

Maybe you have a big obstacle in your path. You need to give God praise first. Praise is what causes things to turn around, what breaks bondages that are holding you back, what activates God's favor. Don't complain. Turn up your praise. "Thank you, Lord, that You have victory in store for Your people. Thank You that You'll get me to where I'm supposed to be." God is going to break through for you. When you give God praise, He doesn't just bring the wall down; He makes a path for you to get to your Promised Land.

Be Encouraged Today:

Praise is what's going to bring the wall down. All through the day, say, "Father, thank You that You're fighting my battles. By Your might I will advance into my promised land."

4 God's Got You

Daniel Delivered from the Lion's Den
Read: Daniel 6:16–23

A young man named Daniel worked for King Darius, who loved him. Daniel was so good at his job that the king was going to put him in charge of his entire empire. However, when the other leaders heard about this, they were jealous and devised a plan to get rid of Daniel.

These leaders tried to manipulate the king by saying, "We wrote a decree that nobody can pray to anyone except you. If they do, they will be thrown into a lion's den." They knew Daniel prayed to Jehovah. They convinced the king to sign the decree and put it into law.

However, this decree didn't change Daniel. Three times a day, just like always, he knelt, opened his windows, and prayed to God. The leaders ran back and told the king that Daniel was defying his order. The king was upset with himself. He knew they had manipulated him, but he couldn't go back on his word, so he had Daniel thrown into a den of lions.

He rescues and he saves; he performs signs and wonders in the heavens and on the earth. He has rescued Daniel from the power of the lions.
Daniel 6:27 (NIV)

When they arrested Daniel and took him to the lion's den, he could have been worried, afraid, or bitter. But Daniel's attitude was, God's got this. I'm in the palm of His hand. Nothing can snatch me away. If it's not my time to go, I'm not going to go. He remained at peace.

What you're facing may be stronger, more powerful than you, and you don't see a way out. But when you refuse to worry and instead stay in peace thanking God that He's in control, by your actions, you're showing God that you're trusting Him.

When the authorities threw Daniel into the lion's den, they expected him to be eaten in a few minutes. These were hungry lions, bred to devour flesh. However, God had miraculously closed the mouths of these lions, making Daniel unappetizing.

When the king saw Daniel coming toward him, passing by the lions, he couldn't believe it. He was overjoyed. The Bible says, *"Not a scratch was found on him, for he had trusted in his God"* (Daniel 6:23, NLT).

Amazing things will happen when you stay in peace. Daniel's faith didn't keep him out of the lion's den, but his faith did make him lion-proof. His faith made it possible for a miracle. God has you in the palm of His hand. Enemies may come against you, but He's placed you out of reach. Like Daniel, He's made you lion-proof.

Be Encouraged Today:

How about you change your perspective and switch over to faith? God is a God of miracles, and He's got you.

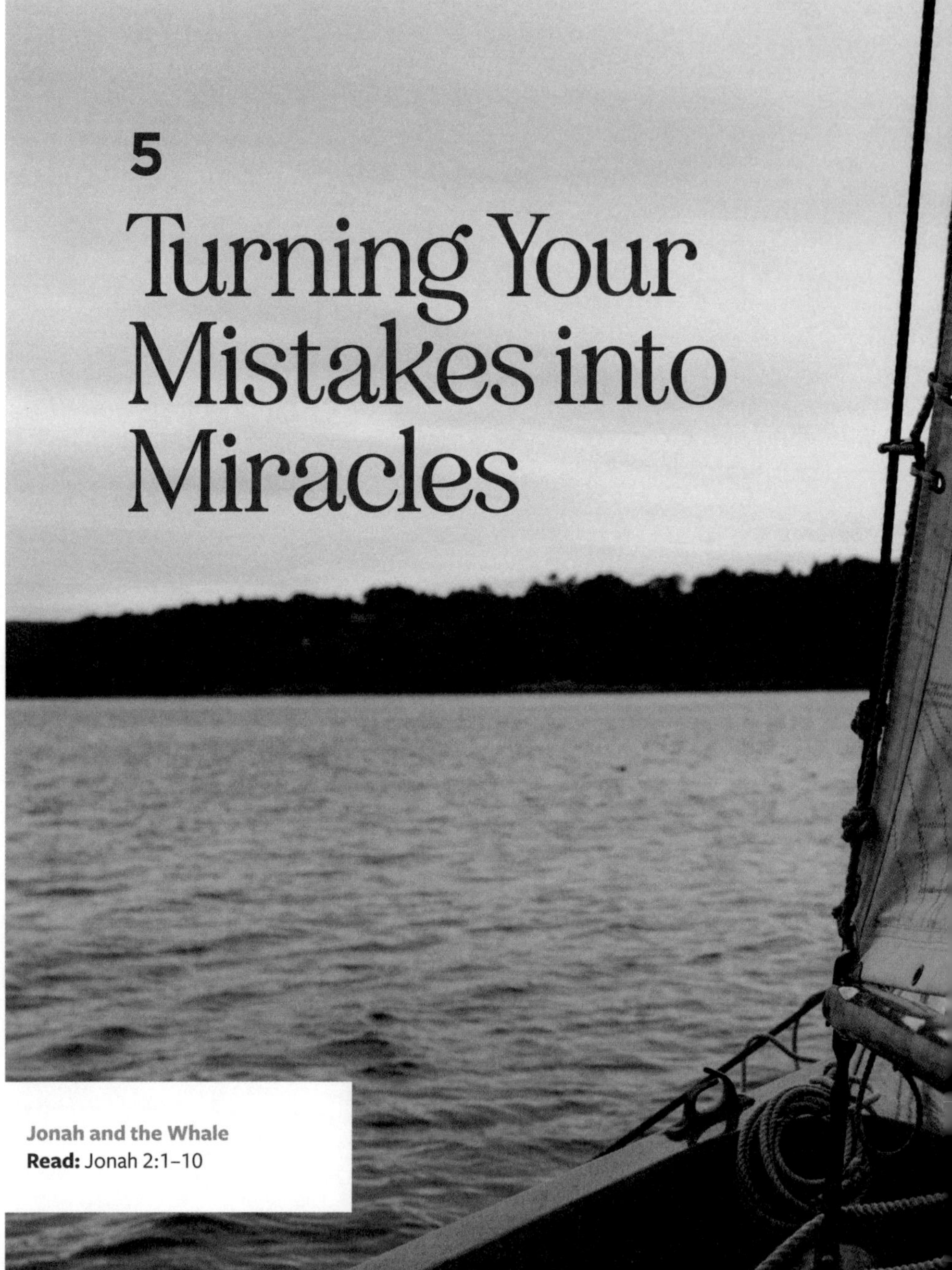

5
Turning Your Mistakes into Miracles

Jonah and the Whale
Read: Jonah 2:1–10

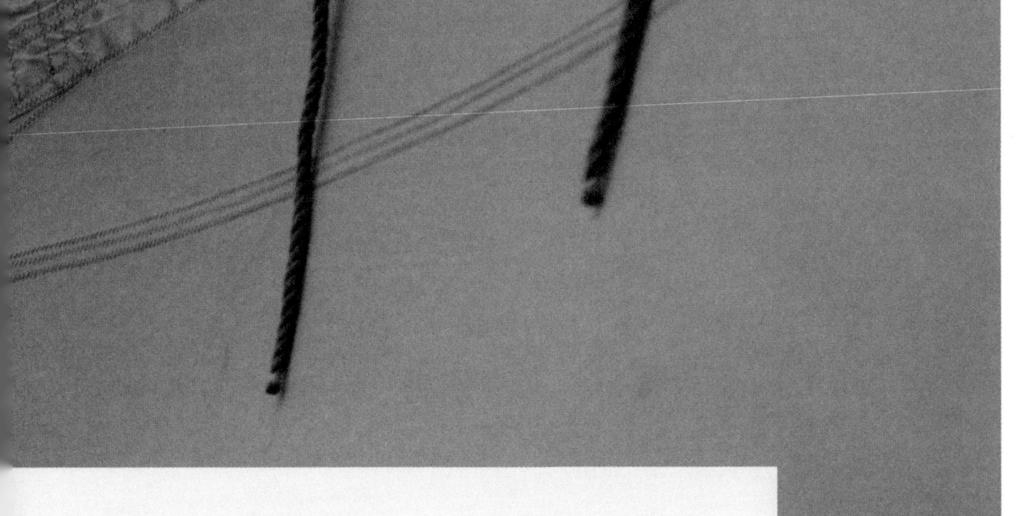

God gave Jonah clear instructions to go to the city of Nineveh, but Jonah didn't want to go. Instead, he ran from God, or so he thought. He boarded a boat headed in the opposite direction, to the farthest port west.

In Jonah 1:4, it says, *"But the LORD hurled a powerful wind over the sea, causing a violent storm that threatened to break the ship apart"* (NLT). It's interesting that the Lord sent the storm. God knows how to get our attention. When you know you're going the wrong way, like the boat, things start to fall apart. God loves you too much to let you miss your destiny. Sometimes we bring the storms on ourselves. If we would just get back on the right course and do what we know to do, the storm would calm down.

The people sailing with Jonah asked, "Who is responsible for causing all this trouble?" Jonah said, "It's me. I know where I'm supposed to be going, but I'm running from the Lord." So, they threw Jonah overboard and the storm died down. Our decisions don't just affect us; they affect our family, our children, and our friends.

I call on the LORD in my distress, and he answers me.
Psalm 120:1 (NIV)

When they threw Jonah overboard, a huge fish swallowed Jonah whole. God, in His great mercy, was saying, "Jonah, you can run, but you can't hide. I'm not finished with you. You have a destiny to fulfill."

Jonah was sitting in the belly of a whale, grateful to be alive. He knew that was the mercy of God having a fish there waiting for him. When you're in the middle of the Mediterranean with no boat, you'll be thankful for a smelly fish. Three days later, that fish spit Jonah up on dry ground.

God made a miracle out of Jonah's mistake.

When you don't follow God's commands, like Jonah, you get off course. But God doesn't give up on you. He simply says,

"recalculating route" like the GPS in your phone. He already has a new way to get you to your destination.

David said, *"The LORD directs the steps of the godly. ... Though they stumble, they will never fall, for the Lord holds them by the hand"* (Psalm 37:23-24, NKJV).

Be Encouraged Today:

Even though God is directing your steps, there will be times that you fall, make mistakes, and go the wrong way. Just like with Jonah, He'll be right there to pick you up. He'll help you get back on the right path.

6

In the Heat Is Your Miracle

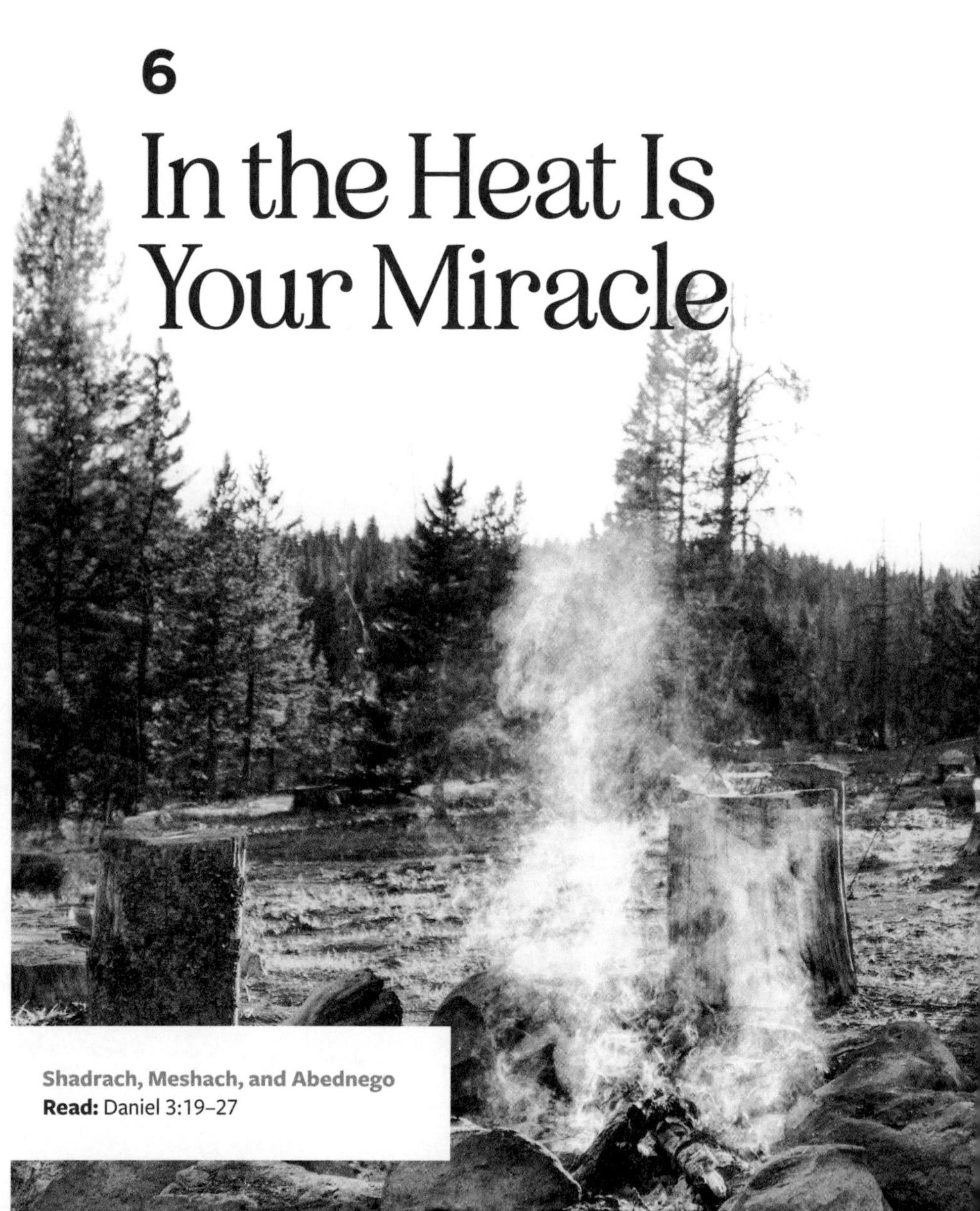

Shadrach, Meshach, and Abednego
Read: Daniel 3:19–27

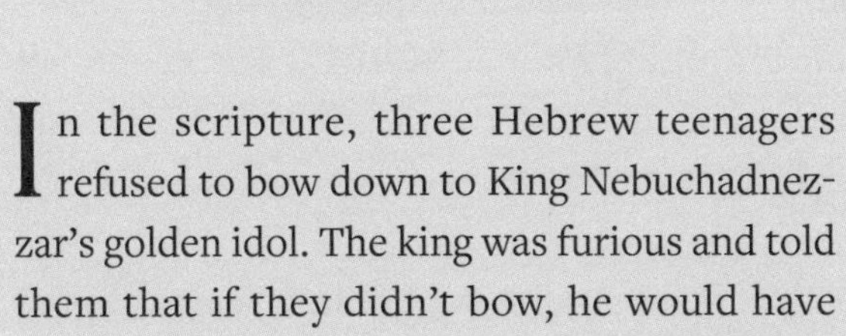

In the scripture, three Hebrew teenagers refused to bow down to King Nebuchadnezzar's golden idol. The king was furious and told them that if they didn't bow, he would have them thrown into a fiery furnace. They refused.

The guards tied up the hands and feet of the teenagers and threw them into the furnace. The fire was so hot that the guards were burned bringing them in. The king looked in the furnace window and said, "Didn't we throw in three bound men? I see four men loosed, and one looks like the Son of God."

What's interesting is that the teenagers couldn't see the fourth man, only those on the outside. When you're in the fire, you may not see God or what He is doing. But you can be sure the fourth man is in there with you. The beauty of our God is that He never lets you go into the fire alone.

The king couldn't believe it. He had them brought out, and the first thing he said was, "From now on, we're all going to worship the God of Shadrach, Meshach, and Abednego." Sometimes you go through the fire so other people will see the hand of God on your life. That the cancer couldn't take you out, the bad break didn't defeat you, the betrayal didn't stop your destiny.

Then you put a leader over us. We went through fire and flood, but you brought us to a place of great abundance.
Psalm 66:12 (NLT)

The scripture says in Daniel 3:30, *"Then the king promoted Shadrach, Meshach, and Abednego to even higher positions in the province of Babylon"* (NLT). The enemy set it up to destroy them, but God turned it into a miracle and used the fire to promote them.

You may feel like you're in a fire right now. It seems like the sickness, the trouble, the bad break is going to limit your life. What you can't see is that there's a fourth man in that fire with you. When you come out, people are going to see you differently.

He knows how much fire, heat, and pressure you can handle. If that fire was going to take you out, He wouldn't have allowed it. It's releasing you into new levels. The fire is all

part of God's plan so you can become everything you were created to be.

I can't promise you that you'll never go through a fire, but I can promise you that you're in a controlled burn. When you're under pressure, God's up to something. God said He's going to bring you through the fire without the smell of smoke.

Be Encouraged Today:

You may be tempted to get upset or scared, but trust Him amid the fire. Remember, there is a fourth Man in there with you. He may not keep you from the fire, but He will make you fireproof. My challenge to you is to stay faithful in the fire because, in the heat, there is a miracle coming.

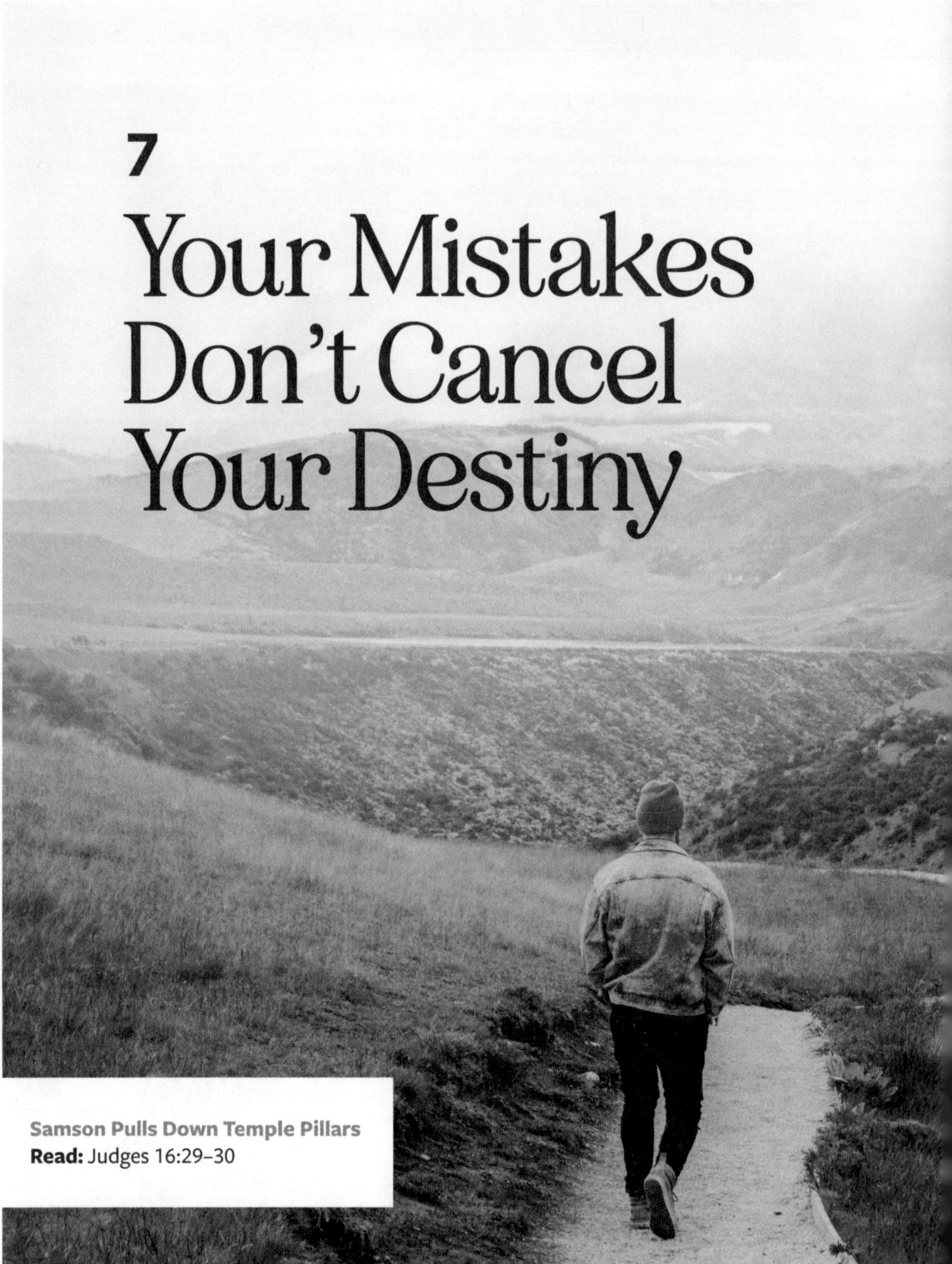

7 Your Mistakes Don't Cancel Your Destiny

Samson Pulls Down Temple Pillars
Read: Judges 16:29–30

The Bible tells the story of an unusual man named Samson who made many mistakes yet was used by God. There were many supernatural occurrences in his life. His birth was predicted by the prophets, and an angel told his mother she would have a child who would be a deliverer and do great things. Samson had supernatural strength, and his enemies couldn't defeat him.

As time passed, he began to let his guard down and started compromising. This once powerful, influential man ended up captured by his enemies. They gouged his eyes out and imprisoned him. Every day he worked as a slave, moving the big grindstone at the mill, chained to it like an animal.

With all his poor choices, you might think God would be done with him. Samson had failed miserably, but God always gives us another chance. Your mistakes don't have to cancel your destiny. After each of Samson's mistakes and compromises and giving in to temptation, the scripture says that the Spirit of the Lord *"strengthened Samson one more time"* (see Judges 16:28).

So now there is no condemnation for those who belong to Christ Jesus.
Romans 8:1 (NLT)

One day his captors were having a big reception in the temple. They brought Samson out to make fun of him. As he was standing there being mocked and ridiculed, Samson asked a young boy to place his hands on the big columns that held up the temple. The miracle was that God had given Samson his strength back one more time. He pushed over the column pillars so the whole building collapsed. Samson defeated more of his enemies in his death than he did in his entire lifetime.

You may have failed again, and the accuser is telling you that you've made too many mistakes, and now you're finished. Like Samson, God has a "one more time" for you. Don't believe what the accuser is telling you.

Romans 8:1 (NIV) says, *"Therefore, there is now no condemnation to those who are in Christ Jesus,"* but here's the key:

"who do not walk according to the flesh but according to the Spirit" (v. 4, NKJV). If you're in the flesh and you make a mistake, ask God for forgiveness, and get up and continue in what God has called you to do. He is faithful to always forgive us of our sins.

You can't go by your feelings; you must go by what you know. You may not feel forgiven, but I know you are forgiven because God's Word says so.

The real question is, are you going to get back in the game? Are you going to get your passion back, your fire back, your dreams back? We have all made mistakes, but God is saying you're forgiven. If He forgives you, why don't you forgive yourself?

Be Encouraged Today:

Your mistakes don't have to cancel your destiny. Say goodbye to guilt and condemnation, dismiss the accusing voices, and get ready for your "one more time." God has something big coming your way, something more rewarding than you've ever seen. This is a new day, and a miracle is possible for you.

8
Special Strength Is Coming

Transfiguration of Christ
Read: Matthew 17:1–6

Before Jesus was crucified, He went up a high mountain with Peter, James, and John. Jesus' appearance changed; His face shone like the sun, and His clothing became dazzling white. Suddenly, Moses and Elijah appeared on the Mount of Transfiguration with Jesus and started talking with Him.

It's interesting that Moses and Elijah were chosen to join Jesus. There were other great heroes of faith who could have been there. Jesus was about to face hardship and suffering, things that were very difficult, even overwhelming and exhausting. Maybe Elijah was there because, even though he had performed great miracles and called down fire from heaven, there was a point when he was too weary to move forward. God had to refresh him and sent angels to give him strength.

We don't know what the conversation was about. Perhaps Elijah encouraged Jesus, telling Him that God would give Him special strength and that angels would be there to minister to Him. Maybe Moses reminded Jesus how, when he was fatigued and too tired to hold up his hands, God sent people to hold his arms up for him. The Father would send people to help lift Jesus up when He fell, to help Him carry the weight of the cross.

...and He was transfigured before them. His face shone like the sun, and His clothes became as white as the light.
Matthew 17:2 (NKJV)

When you face times where you feel fatigued, be encouraged. You were never meant to act in your own strength. Like Moses and Elijah, who didn't think they could go on, God sent help to strengthen them. God has angels to strengthen you and the right people to help you. God is not going to let you miss your destiny.

He gives strength to the weary, and He will strengthen you. Even Jesus fell under the weight of the cross. Sometimes your cross is too heavy to carry by yourself. Like Jesus, you may fall, but God will always have a Simon there, someone to help you carry it.

Be Encouraged Today:

When you are weak, He is strong. You're going to think, *Where did I get this energy, this power, this ability?* That's the miracle — God giving you special strength. You are strong; you are victorious; you are well able with God's help.

9
"Net-Breaking" Blessings

The Miraculous Catch of Fish
Read: Luke 5:1–11

When Jesus finished teaching the crowd by the Sea of Galilee, He told Peter to launch back out into the deep, promising that he would catch a great haul of fish. Peter, a professional fisherman who had fished all night and caught nothing, initially doubted Jesus' instruction. As a teacher and Rabbi, Jesus seemed out of place giving fishing advice. However, Peter decided to obey, saying in effect, "Jesus, this doesn't make sense to me, but nevertheless, at your word, I'm going to do it." He went out and caught so many fish that his nets began to break, requiring another boat to help, and both boats were so loaded down that they were about to sink.

What's interesting is that there were no fish in that spot a couple of hours before, and they had fished all night. However, God controls the fish. He knows where your provision is and how to get it to you, even if it doesn't make sense or seem logical. God often works in extraordinary and uncommon ways to show His hand.

Let them shout for joy and be glad, who favor my righteous cause; and let them say continually, "Let the LORD be magnified, who has pleasure in the prosperity of His servant."
Psalm 35:27 (NKJV)

Earlier, Peter had let Jesus borrow his boat, which was not only his business but also his source of income. Peter could have refused, but he generously gave his resource to Jesus, symbolizing putting God first. Proverbs 3:9 says, *"Honor the Lord with your wealth, with the first fruits of all your crops. Then your barns will be filled to overflowing, and your vats will brim over with new wine"* (NIV).

If you want to see supernatural provision, you must be a giver. Honor God with your first fruits, the first part of your income, and invite Him into your business. When you give God your resources, you set yourself up for overflow and abundance. Giving is like sowing a seed: You can't give to God without Him giving you more in return. Peter owned the boat, but God owned the sea. God controls the universe, and when you let Him use your resources, He'll cause blessings to overflow in your life.

The scripture says that when you give, it will be given back to you, but not in the same manner. Instead, it will be pressed down, shaken together, and running over (see Luke 6:38). Our God is a 'net-breaking' God. You may have worked hard and honored God but still come up empty. However, your time is coming. God is directing blessings your way, blessings that are so abundant they will overflow to future generations. You'll have to call in more boats to take in all the overflow.

Be Encouraged Today:

God has supernatural provision for you, and you can go from having nothing to having nets full of blessings. Instead of focusing on the size of the lack, the debt, or the struggle, look at how big your God is. Shift your perspective and get ready for overflow.

10
Roll Away Your Stone

Lazarus Raised from the Dead
Read: John 11:38–44

In John 11, there is an account where Jesus hears that his good friend Lazarus is very sick. Lazarus was in another city, and they wanted Jesus to come and pray for him. For some reason, Jesus was delayed for two days, and Lazarus ended up dying. Jesus said to his disciples, "Our friend Lazarus has fallen asleep, but I am going there to wake him up."

Though Lazarus was clearly dead, Jesus had a different perspective; He said Lazarus was only asleep. Could it be that what you think is dead — that relationship, that dream — is really just asleep like Lazarus? All the circumstances say it's over, but God says, "Don't worry, I have a different perspective. It's not dead; it's only asleep." God is about to wake up what you think is dead.

Four days later, Jesus showed up at Lazarus' house. He had been in the tomb so long that the body smelled badly. You may have situations in your life that stink — your marriage, your finances, a ruined relationship, that mistake you made that messed up your life. In its current state, your life stinks. Jesus went to the tomb and told the men to roll away the stone. Martha warned him, "*...by this time there's a stench. He's been dead four days!*" (John 11:39, MSG).

Then he said to me, "Speak a prophetic message to these bones and say, 'Dry bones, listen to the word of the Lord! This is what the Sovereign Lord says: Look! I am going to put breath into you and make you live again!'"
Ezekiel 37:4-5 (NLT)

God went to where the stink was. Sometimes we think God will only help us if we've lived perfectly and everything smells good, but God goes to the stinky places in our lives. God is encouraging you to let Him in. He can wake up the healing, wake up the restoration, wake up the new beginning. God is inviting you to roll away the stone. The smell doesn't bother Him. God goes where the mess is — where you were betrayed, where you lost a loved one, where you compromised. You said you wouldn't do it anymore, but you failed again. Now it stinks and you feel disqualified. That stink is just temporary. That dream is not dead; it's just asleep.

Ezekiel saw a valley of dead bones, and God told him to speak to them: "Dry bones, listen to the Word of the Lord. I will breathe into you and make you come alive." Ezekiel did just that, and that army of dry bones came to life.

Listen to the Word of the Lord because those bones that appeared dead are about to wake up. Perhaps you think like Mary and Martha, There's no way it could happen now. Get ready; it's not too late, it's not too far gone. God is about to do a miracle and awaken something in you and in your life.

Be Encouraged Today:

I believe things you've given up on, perhaps considered dead like Lazarus, are about to wake up — dreams, healing, marriages, and breakthroughs are waking up.

11

God's Goodness Test

God Provides Manna
Read: Exodus 16:14–35

In Deuteronomy 8, God told the Israelites that He was bringing them into the Promised Land. It was described as a land of abundance, flowing with streams and rivers where the cluster of grapes was so big it took two people to carry them.

After promising them all this favor and blessing, God gave them a warning. He said in verses 11-16, *"Beware that in your plenty you do not forget the* Lord *your God. . . . . For when you have become full and prosperous and have built fine homes to live in, ... your silver and gold have multiplied, . . . Do not forget . . . the* Lord *your God, who rescued you out of slavery . . . Do not forget that he led you through the great and terrifying wilderness with its poisonous snakes . . . He gave you water from the rock! He fed you with manna in the wilderness, a food unknown to your ancestors"* (NLT). This was a test. Four times God cautioned them not to forget the source of all these blessings.

He fed you with manna in the wilderness, a food unknown to your ancestors. He did this to humble you and test you for your own good.
Deuteronomy 8:16 (NLT)

God's supernatural provision of food in the desert for so many Israelites was a miracle. God miraculously fed them with manna, which means 'what is it?'. They had never seen manna before. It was bread that mysteriously formed on the ground every morning.

God has some 'what is it?' for you too. Something you've never seen before. Things you don't understand, opportunities you never imagined. Things are about to shift in your favor. Unexpected opportunities, healings, or breakthroughs are suddenly going to happen because God is preparing manna for you. He's getting things ready to take you where you couldn't go on your own.

When you see this miracle manna, the favor that you've not seen before, always remember that it is the Lord your God causing you to increase. If you will start recognizing God's favor, thanking Him for what He's done, living from a place of gratitude, then He will open new doors and take you even further than you've imagined. God won't share the credit,

but when you're quick to give Him the credit, there's no limit to how high you will go.

Recognize His goodness in your life. Remember how He led you through the desert, providing the mysterious manna for so many years, and brought you into the land of milk and honey. Remember how He brought you out of that problem and opened that door. Don't forget, it was the Lord your God. He has been working behind the scenes in your life, even generations back.

Be Encouraged Today:

Get up every morning and say, "Lord, I'm so grateful. Thank You for Your goodness." You will see something that you've never seen before: new levels of favor, influence, anointing, and creativity.

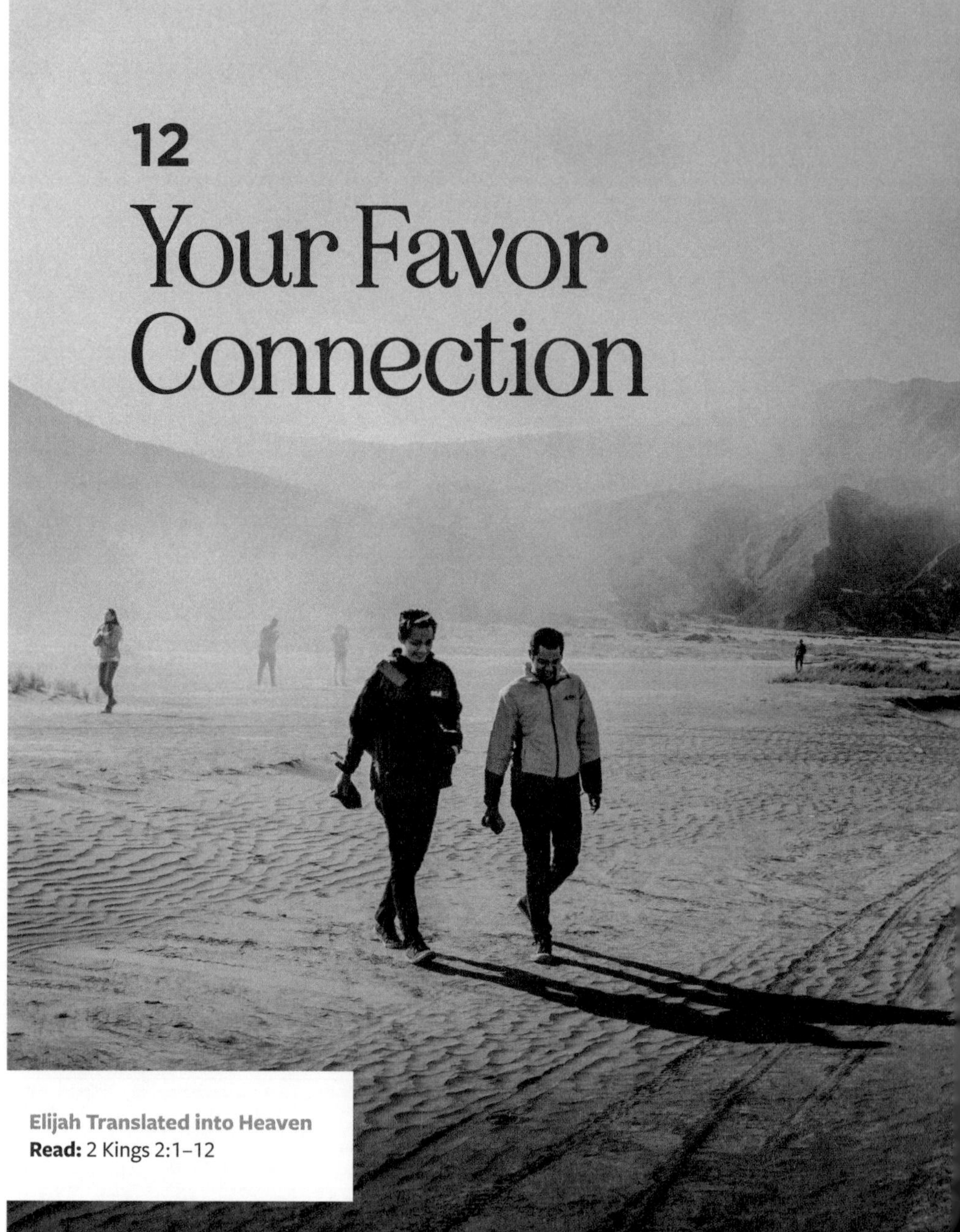

12
Your Favor Connection

Elijah Translated into Heaven
Read: 2 Kings 2:1–12

Elijah was a mighty prophet who performed amazing miracles. He called down fire from heaven and raised a little girl from the dead and out ran a chariot. One day, while walking by a field, he saw a young man named Elisha plowing. He told him to leave his animals and come with him. Elisha, who was from a wealthy family, likely had dreams and goals of his own. Elijah wanted him to be his assistant, bringing him food, setting up his tent, and feeding his animals. Elisha could have thought, *No thanks, I'm going to stay here and work on my farm.* He could have been too proud, but he recognized the favor on Elijah's life and respected his anointing.

Elisha wasn't jealous. He didn't get offended at being offered what seemed like a low-level position. For years, he served Elijah with honor, making him comfortable and waiting on him. When you honor those whom God has given influence and esteem, that honor and influence will come back to you.

I'm sure Elisha's friends came around, saying, "Why are you still serving this old man? You have your own dreams. He's holding you back." He could have let them talk him out of it, thinking he was wasting his time. Instead, he kept on serving, honoring, and respecting the 'favor connection.' Elijah was miraculously taken to Heaven in a whirlwind. But there is another miracle here. Elisha, the assistant who served faithfully all those years, received a double portion of Elijah's anointing.

Do not be deceived, God is not mocked; for whatever a man sows, that he will also reap.
Galatians 6:7 (NLT)

These 'favor connections' you're sowing into, honoring, and serving are not a waste of time. It is a Biblical principle: What you sow into, you're going to reap. When you sow into someone with great favor, you're going to reap some of that favor. Like Elisha, you'll see double the influence, double the favor, double the anointing.

It's very freeing when you can celebrate people ahead of you, knowing that the seeds you have sown into them — the honor, the respect, the resources — will bring a harvest for you. If you only sow into horizontal relationships, people at your same level, then you'll see horizontal favor. But when you're secure enough in who you are to recognize the

favor on people's lives and sow into vertical relationships, people who are ahead of you, then you'll reap some of that vertical favor.

God has brought people into your life not to compete with but to connect with. They're a key to you rising higher. This is not about playing up to people and trying to win them over; it's about recognizing and respecting the favor God has placed on people.

Be Encouraged Today:

Connect with people that are seeing favor; celebrate them, honor them, cheer them on because that connection to favor will reap favor for you.

13

You Are Invisible to the Enemy

Syrian Army is Blinded
Read: 2 Kings 6:18–20

God has a ring of protection around you, a bloodline that the enemy cannot cross. God knows how to make you invisible to the enemy. The same God who made blind eyes see can make seeing eyes blind. He has many ways to protect you. That's what happened in 2 Kings, chapter 6.

The Syrian army surrounded Elijah's house because God kept revealing their plans to him. When the Syrian king found out, he sent a huge army to capture Elijah. Elijah prayed for the army to be blinded and then led them straight to the Israelite camp. When their eyes were opened, they realized they had been captured. God has ways to protect you that you've never thought of. He can make you invisible to the enemy of your soul.

In the Red Sea is a small flounder fish called a Moses Sole, as well as large sharks. These sharks typically prey on small fish. However, researchers noticed something fascinating about this little flounder. While all the other small fish of the same size and weight would be eaten by the sharks, the sharks weren't eating this Moses Sole. They discovered the Moses Sole has a unique defense system. When it's in any kind of danger, it secretes poisonous toxins from its glands. These toxins cause the shark's jaw to freeze, and they can't bite or swallow the fish.

Those who live in the shelter of the Most High will find rest in the shadow of the Almighty. This I declare about the LORD: He alone is my refuge, my place of safety; he is my God, and I trust him. For he will rescue you from every trap and protect you from deadly disease. He will cover you with his feathers. He will shelter you with his wings. His faithful promises are your armor and protection.
Psalm 91:1–4 (NLT)

Like this small fish, as a child of God, He has put something on you that will keep the enemy from biting and devouring you. What you're up against may seem big and powerful. Don't worry; it can't touch you. God is protecting you. He has given you a way to release power that causes the enemy's jaws to freeze — by praising and thanking Him. Every time you say, "Lord, thank You that You're my shield. Thank You that You're my defender. Thank You that You're the Guardian of my soul," that power is released. Faith-filled thanksgiving is toxic to your enemies and paralyzes them.

Negative talk is like shark bait that attracts the enemy. The way you activate God's protection is with praise and faith-filled words. Think about the little Moses Soul. When it's in the shark's mouth, it doesn't get depressed and think, *This is the end.* It just goes about its business, knowing there's something special about it. So, it just rests in who God made it to be.

The Most-High God is the guardian of your soul. He's put something on you that makes you untouchable to the enemy. Live in a place of peace, a place of faith, knowing that God is watching and guarding you. If you'll do this, God will rescue you from every trap, protect you from every plague, and make you invisible to the enemy.

Be Encouraged Today:

Stay in the secret place, safe in the presence of God, thanking Him for protecting you, defending you. He will be the guardian of your soul, making you invisible to the enemy.

14
Your Best Is Next

Water Turned to Wine
Read: John 2:1–11

In John 2, Jesus attended a wedding in Galilee, a multi-day celebration with hundreds of guests. However, the joyous occasion took a turn when they ran out of wine. Jesus instructed the staff to fill six large water pots with water. When the pots were filled, He told them to draw some out and take it to the master of the feast. To everyone's amazement, the water had been turned into the finest wine.

If the wine had not run out, they would have never seen the best wine. God saves the best for next. You may feel like you're coming to an end. You're running out — of opportunity, favor, resources, or strength. This may sound odd, but you're in a good place. When you come to the end, that's when God steps in and doesn't just help you get through it, but brings out the best for next.

The best position, the best relationships, the best in your finances, the best in your health, the best in your family are coming. The fact that things are running out doesn't mean that God has forgotten about you or that you are done. It's a sign that God is about to do something you've never seen before.

"You're blessed when you're at the end of your rope. With less of you there is more of God and his rule."
Matthew 5:3 (MSG)

There are seasons that come to an end; you run out of a good thing. The first wine the people had was fine, but the wine was supposed to run out. It was a part of God's plan. If it didn't run out, they would have never seen the best wine.

What runs out in your life is not a surprise to God. You're going to look back and say like that host, "You've saved the best for now." When you see the new door God opens and how He promotes you in the presence of your enemies and how He gives you influence and favor that you've never seen, you'll say, "Thank You, Lord. You saved the best for now."

Don't be discouraged when something runs out; keep the right perspective. God loves you too much and is too generous to leave you with just "what's good enough." At some point, that will come to an end so He can bring to your life

the best. That's what "He's taking you from glory to glory" means. In between those glories, there will be seasons where you'll feel like you have no more.

Jesus said in Matthew 5:3, *"You're blessed when you're at the end of your rope. With less of you, there is more of God and His rule"* (MSG). We're blessed when we're at the end of ourselves or the season we are in. When you've run out of options, that's when God does a miracle and gives you something better, better than you can imagine.

Be Encouraged Today:

When you feel you've come to the end, that's when God steps in to show you He's saved the best for next.

15
Keep on Walking

Healing of the Ten Lepers
Read: Luke 17:11–19

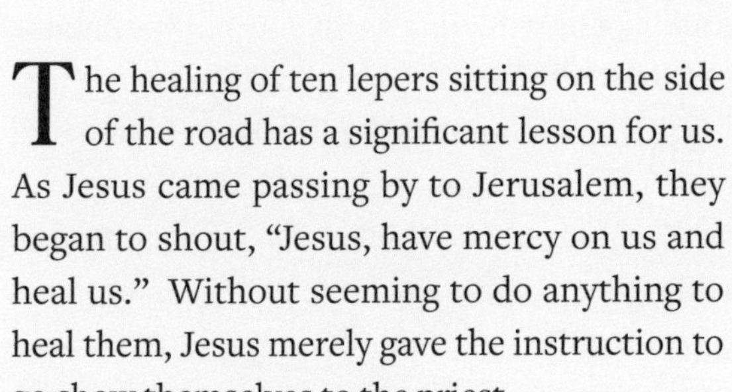

The healing of ten lepers sitting on the side of the road has a significant lesson for us. As Jesus came passing by to Jerusalem, they began to shout, "Jesus, have mercy on us and heal us." Without seeming to do anything to heal them, Jesus merely gave the instruction to go show themselves to the priest.

They could have thought, *Once I see my skin clear up, I'll go see the priest.* But faith says you must believe it before you see it. You must act like it's coming when you don't see any sign of it. These lepers obeyed Jesus in blind faith and started walking toward the priest. It could have been several miles, perhaps all day. I can hear people saying, "You can't go into town; you have leprosy."

They could have looked at their skin and thought, *I don't see anything different,* but they just kept on walking. No sign of things improving or changes in their skin, but hour after hour they kept walking. Scripture shares that as they went, they were healed. If they would have stayed where they were, waited for things to change, they would have never seen the healing. The miracle was in the obedience, in the going. By the time they got to the priest, they were all completely healed.

Once I was young, and now I am old. Yet I have never seen the godly abandoned or their children begging for bread.
Psalm 37:25 (NLT)

God has put promises in your heart. Perhaps He's told you He is going to restore your health, that you will lend and not borrow, that as for you and your house you will serve the Lord. However, like these lepers, nothing looks any different. The medical report hasn't changed, your child is still off course, your business hasn't improved. You could get discouraged and think, *I don't see any change.* Just keep walking, keep being obedient, keep praising, keep thanking, keep doing the right thing. That's when the miracle is going to take place.

You can't go by what you see or by what you don't see; go by what God has promised you. "Joel, I still have these symptoms." Keep on walking. "My business is still slow." Keep on walking. "These people at work are still not treating me right." Keep on walking. God sees your obedience. He sees you believing when you could be discouraged, He hears you praising when you could be complaining, He sees you stretching forward when you could be shrinking back. As you keep walking, you're going to see God do miraculous things in your life.

This miracle required an act of obedience. These lepers had to do something as an act of faith — which was see the priest — and when they did, they were healed.

Be Encouraged Today:

If you don't see anything changing, keep walking. Keep being obedient, keep praising, keep thanking, keep doing the right thing. That's when the miracle is going to take place.

16

Tapping into God's Power

Jesus' Resurrection
Read: Luke 24:6

I want to tell you about the power that's available to us because of the resurrection of Jesus Christ. Paul said in Philippians 3:10, *"I want to know Christ and experience the mighty power that raised him from the dead"* (NLT).

So many people go around feeling weak and defeated, always struggling under their circumstances. But God did not create us to be weaklings.

Over 2000 years ago, a baby was born in a manger. He brought hope and healing, despite being hated by the world. Nailed to the cross, it seemed like the end, but Jesus fought darkness for three days, triumphing over evil. Satan was no match; *"Jesus crushed Satan's head"* (see Genesis 3:15). Jesus defeated and dethroned our eternal enemy once and for all.

Placed in a tomb on Friday, He emerged victorious on Sunday, proclaiming, "I am He who lives, I was dead, but I am alive forever more," adding, "I've got the keys to death and hell."

I also pray that you will understand the incredible greatness of God's power for us who believe him. This is the same mighty power that raised Christ from the dead and seated him in the place of honor at God's right hand in the heavenly realms.
Ephesians 1:19–20 (NLT)

God has already triumphed over death and the grave for us all. Now we don't have to be afraid. It's time to start tapping into God's power.

Years ago, we knew a man from Alaska whose family had deep, generational roots in the occult and witchcraft. His father, a cult leader, claimed to leave his body and traverse the spirit world.

One night, he attempted to cast a spell on someone's home but found it impenetrable. Peering through a window, he saw Believers glowing brightly, engaging in what appeared to be a Bible study. This impenetrable light kept him at bay. He later told his son, "If believers truly understood their spiritual power, they would never be afraid again."

In light of the incredible victory and power demonstrated through Jesus' resurrection, let us awaken to the truth of our spiritual inheritance. Just as Jesus defeated darkness and evil, we too can conquer fear and negativity by tapping into God's resurrection power within us.

When faced with challenges that seem insurmountable, remember the victory that Jesus secured for us. Let go of fear and doubt, and instead, boldly declare His authority over every obstacle. Stay anchored in faith, keep believing, and tap into His resurrection power.

Perhaps you are in a situation that, in the natural, looks as good as dead. Your business may have declined, or your hope may have died, leaving you feeling afraid and powerless. Remember, you possess incredible power within — the same power that raised Jesus from the dead is available to you if you'll simply start believing.

Be Encouraged Today:

As you align your thoughts and actions with God's promises, anticipate the miraculous resurrection of what seems dead in your life. Trust that God is breathing new life into every situation. Your resurrection miracle is on the horizon — embrace it with unwavering faith and expectation.

17
Let Your Faith Show

Paul Heals the Lame Man
Read: Acts 14:10

In Acts 14, as Paul was teaching the people, he noticed a man in the crowd. This man had been crippled since birth and had never known what it was like to walk. Verse 9 says, *"Paul realized he had faith to be healed"* (NLT). As the man was sitting and listening to Paul, he must have had such anticipation on his face that Paul noticed. Paul could see something in his expression, an expectancy that something good was about to happen. Paul was so impressed with his expression that he stopped his message and said, "Sir, I can see you're ready for a miracle. Stand up." The man stood up, was instantly healed, and began to walk for the very first time.

Like this man, we should live with expectancy and anticipation. Yes, we all face difficulties, challenges, disappointments, or have reasons to be sour, but don't let them talk you out of what God wants to do. There is something amazing in your future. Can people sense your faith? Can others notice that you're expecting to go to a new level? Are you talking, thinking, and acting like it's going to happen? The Bible says we walk by faith (2 Corinthians 5:7). There should be an expectancy in the way we talk and behave.

And he said to her, "Daughter, your faith has made you well. Go in peace. Your suffering is over."
Mark 5:34 (NLT)

The answer to your prayer could happen this week. You could see your health turn around this month. This could be your year, where things fall into place and promises you've been believing for a while suddenly come to pass. When you live with expectancy, where your faith can be seen in your attitude, your expressions, and how you talk, that's going to cause God to notice you in a new way. God is always with us, but faith is what gets His attention.

The scripture says in Hebrews 11:6, "*without faith it is impossible to please God*" (NIV). That means you can be obedient and not please God. You can give, love others, help the poor, and volunteer; those things are great, and we should do them all. But if you're not believing, declaring things unseen, and thanking Him that He's bringing promises to pass, then you're not walking by faith.

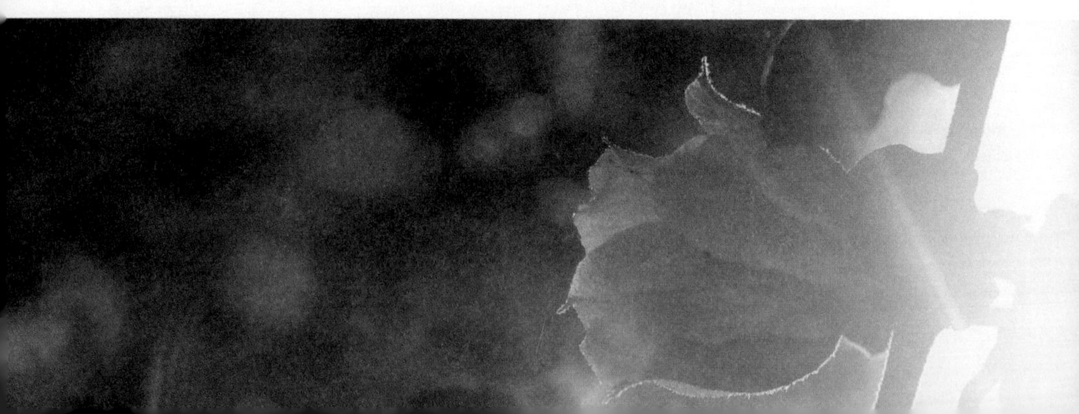

The woman with the issue of blood wasn't passive. She acted in faith and believed that when she touched the hem of His robe, she would be healed. Jesus said to her, "Your faith has made you well." Don't just watch as Jesus passes by. Reach out to Him with anticipation that He is going to touch you. Act and speak like that woman in faith. "Father, thank You that You're healing me. Thank You that You're taking me where I can't go on my own." That's how we touch His hem today, through our faith. Thank You that my miracle is on the way!

Be Encouraged Today:

God is about to open supernatural doors and turn impossible situations around. Your faith and expectancy are going to bring freedom, breakthrough, abundance, and the fullness of your destiny, in Jesus' name.

18
Your Victory Begins in the Dark

Earthquake Frees Paul and Silas
Read: Acts 16:25–26

Paul and Silas were put in prison for sharing their faith. The religious Pharisees accused them of causing a disturbance. To ensure they couldn't escape, they were put in the deepest part of the dungeon. Paul and Silas had chains around their feet and guards were stationed nearby. It looked like they would never be heard from again. All odds were against them, but people don't have the final say.

They could have been depressed sitting in that dungeon, falsely accused, thinking, *God, this is so wrong; we are innocent.* The scripture shares that at midnight, they sang praises and gave thanks to God. It's interesting that we're told when this happened. For most other miracles we read about, we don't have the time. But God had the writer tell us the time because midnight signifies the start of a new day.

As they sang praises, a great earthquake suddenly shook the prison, causing the doors to fly open and the chains to fall off their feet. Eventually, they walked out as free men. It's not a coincidence that this all happened at midnight. They might have been singing praises at ten o'clock that evening, and nothing happened, or at eleven o'clock, and still, nothing. But when midnight arrived, signaling the start of a new day, suddenly things changed.

Sing to the LORD, all you godly ones! Praise his holy name. For his anger lasts only a moment, but his favor lasts a lifetime! Weeping may last through the night, but joy comes with the morning. When I was prosperous, I said, "Nothing can stop me now!"
Psalm 30:4–6 (NLT)

God is showing that even when it's dark all around you, and you don't see a way out, when you come into that new day, when you cross from PM to AM, things suddenly shift. There may be a period of darkness where it doesn't look like anything is happening, but if you keep thanking God that He's fighting your battles, thanking Him for making ways where you don't see a way, then God will suddenly show out in your life and surprise you.

You may be facing areas where everything seems dark and stagnant. This is a test. Will you choose to praise Him in the darkness? Will you thank Him, believing that what He promised is on its way? Don't be swayed by your feelings; they may try to convince you that things will never work out. Similarly, your mind may present all the reasons why it won't happen. Instead, walk by faith.

Keep praising Him in the dark, thanking Him, doing good to others, giving, and serving. When you do that, like Paul and Silas, suddenly doors are going to open. Suddenly you're going to come into opportunity, the right people, healing, breakthroughs. It's going to catapult you out of the darkness.

Midnight is a good thing because God often starts working in the dark. That's a sign He's about to birth something new, something big, something unusual. If He began in the light, it wouldn't take any faith. If we could see how it was going happen and we had all the resources, the connections, the solutions, we wouldn't have to depend on Him. Instead of getting depressed, the right attitude is, "Yes, it's still dark. Yes, I don't see anything changing, but I'm not worried. I know it's after midnight, but light is coming." God is faithful. What He promised, He's going to bring to pass.

Be Encouraged Today:

Pray this in faith: "Father, thank You that I've come into my midnight, and it's a new day. Even though it may still be dark, I know You start the day in the dark, and the light is on the way. So, I will keep a song of thanksgiving and praise in my heart."

19

Secure in His Plans for You

Jesus Appears to Saul
Read: Acts 9:3–6

When we are introduced to Saul in the Bible, he is a major adversary of the early church. He obtained letters from the authorities to arrest those who followed Jesus and drag them off to prison. He even stood by and approved when Stephen was stoned to death. At first glance, it might seem like Saul was beyond redemption, that God would have no interest in him. However, we can't anticipate what God has planned. His sovereign will is not thwarted by our decisions.

Saul was on horseback traveling to Damascus with the intention of arresting Believers. His mission was to create more trouble for followers of Jesus. Suddenly, a light from Heaven flashed around him, knocking him to the ground. The encounter was so intense that he was blinded.

A voice thundered, "Saul, Saul, why are you persecuting me?" Saul responded, "Who are you, Lord?" That moment marked a significant turning point. Saul later became Paul, the apostle who authored nearly half of the New Testament. If God's will was solely contingent on Paul's choices, he would not have fulfilled his destiny. The beauty lies in God's sovereign will, which transcends our decisions or ambitions.

"For I know the plans I have for you," says the LORD. "They are plans for good and not for disaster, to give you a future and a hope."
Jeremiah 29:11 (NLT)

It's the goodness of God loving us when we don't deserve it, showing us mercy when we should receive judgment. You may have veered off course, made decisions you're not proud of. You may feel like you're washed up. Can I offer you some encouragement? The Sovereign God is still in control of your life. He's already planned ahead of time these moments of mercy, healing, favor, where He won't just restore you, but He'll thrust you into your purpose.

Paul wrote in Galatians, *"But even before I was born, God chose me and called me by his marvelous grace. Then it pleased him to reveal his Son to me so that I would proclaim the Good News about Jesus to the Gentiles"* (vv. 15-16, NLT). He was essentially saying, "God had already decided in advance to

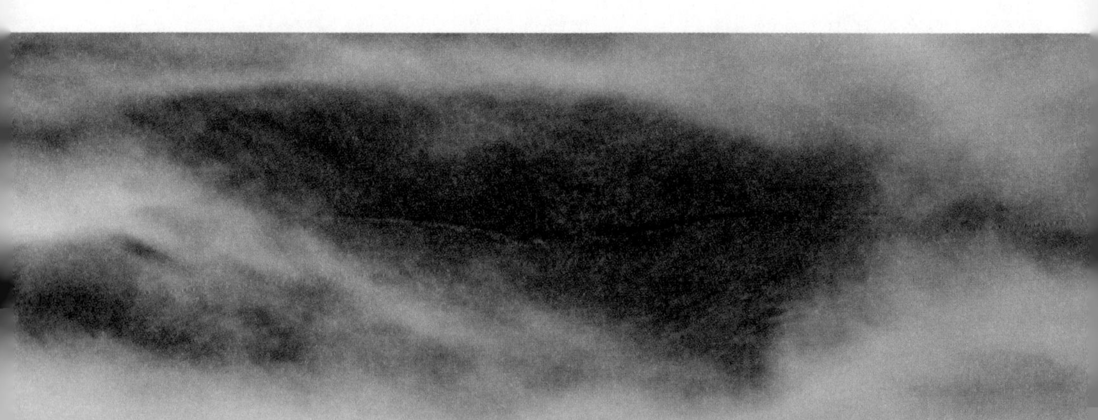

use me to preach the Good News, even though I was doing the opposite." Then the Sovereign God intervened, the God who supersedes our decisions, and set Paul on a path to his destiny.

When you understand that He's Sovereign, that He's not basing everything on your choices, your ability, your background, your family, then you can remain at peace. His sovereign will is unstoppable. Sometimes we get frustrated because we can't see the whole script. We don't know what God is up to. We go through disappointments, loss, bad breaks. Nothing is random; it's all working according to the plans He has for you, what He decided long ago.

Be Encouraged Today:

Trust God, even when you don't understand. Believe that He is a Sovereign God who has a purpose for you. He is going to override your mistakes and thrust you into your destiny.

20
Your Answer Is Coming Sooner Than Expected

Angel Frees Peter
Read: Acts 12:7–11

In Acts 12, King Herod showed hostility toward the church and had a strong dislike for Believers. Consequently, he ordered Peter's arrest and imprisonment. Herod had already executed one of the disciples, James, brother of John. Peter's situation was very serious and urgent. He was held in the most secure part of the prison, chained to two guards. The next day he would be brought to trial. Thankfully, a large group of Believers had gathered at Mary's house and were praying fervently for Peter. They knew the seriousness of the situation, as Peter was just hours away from losing his life.

In the middle of the night, an angel appeared in the prison, waking Peter, and told him, "Get up and come with me." Peter thought it was a dream, but then the chains fell off without a key. They passed by the guards unnoticed and reached an iron gate that seemed impossible to open, but miraculously, it swung open (Acts 12:10).

"It shall come to pass That before they call, I will answer; And while they are still speaking, I will hear."
Isaiah 65:24 (NKJV)

At that moment, Peter realized this wasn't a dream; this was really happening. He hurried to Mary's house, where the believers were gathered in prayer. When he knocked, a young woman named Rhoda answered. When she heard Peter's voice, she was so overjoyed that she ran to tell the others without opening the door. "Peter is at the door! Our prayers have been answered!" she exclaimed.

The response from those praying was one of disbelief. "Rhoda, calm down. Peter can't be at the door. He's in jail, chained up in the dungeon. You must be mistaken," they insisted. But Rhoda remained adamant, saying, "I heard his voice with my own ears. Peter is standing at the door."

Meanwhile, Peter stood outside, knocking, and likely thinking, *Come on. I'm the answer to your prayers; at least let me in.* The Believers had been praying for Peter's release, but the immediacy of the answer seemed to catch them off guard. It was one of those unexpected answers to prayer that they hadn't anticipated could come so quickly.

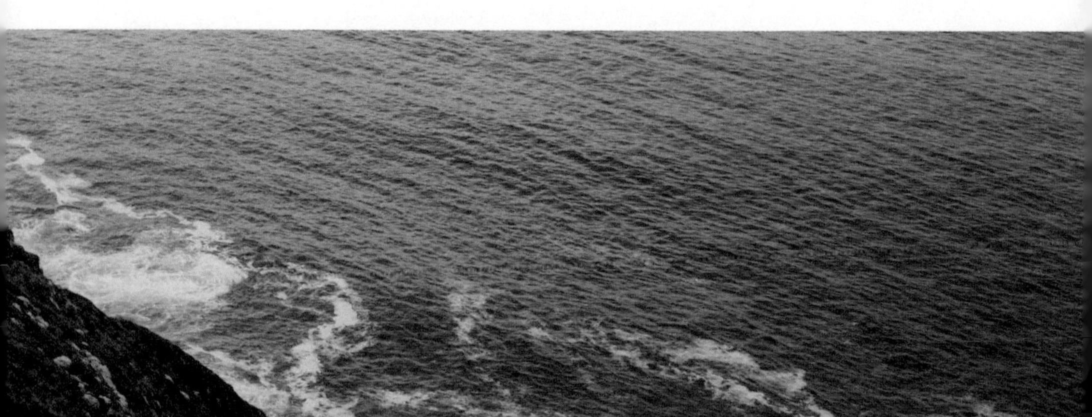

All the circumstances indicated that if Peter ever got out, it would be months or years. I want to encourage you: God has some unexpected deliveries coming your way. He knows how to bring about a solution sooner than you think. Don't repeat the mistake of these Believers and say, "There's no way. Have you seen my circumstances? It's never going to happen." Even when every circumstance seems to suggest otherwise — remember, the chains have already been loosened.

Just like with Peter, God can do it suddenly, unexpectedly, quicker than you thought. While you're still praying about something, the answer is knocking at the door. While you're praying for the breakthrough, the angel has already loosed the chains. God's already set the miracle into motion.

Be Encouraged Today:

Get ready because God is setting the miracle into motion. There's going to be a knock at your door sooner than expected. Your miracle is knocking.

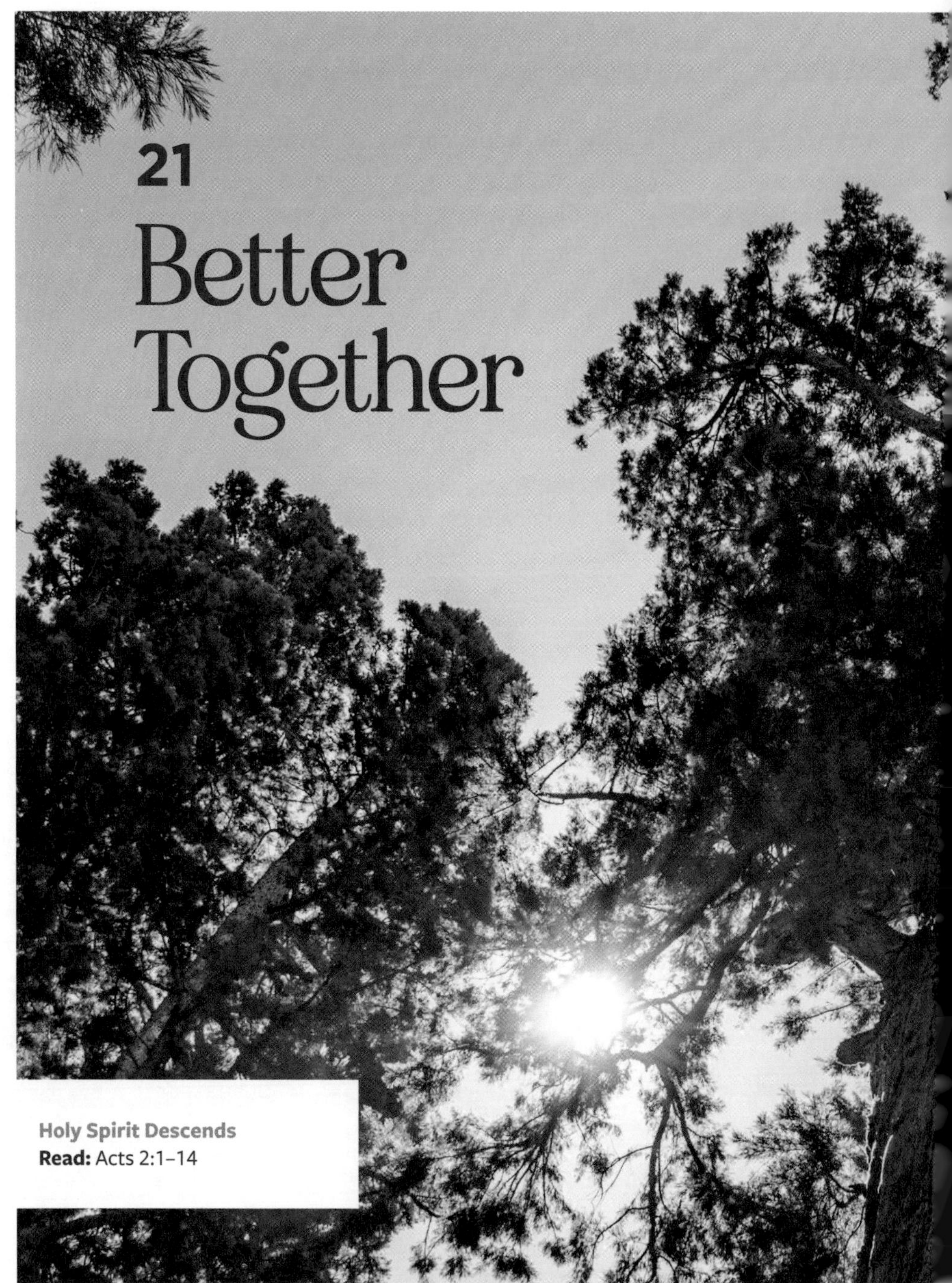

21

Better Together

Holy Spirit Descends
Read: Acts 2:1–14

In Acts 1, Jesus had recently risen from the dead. He instructed His followers not to leave Jerusalem but to wait for the promise of the Holy Spirit. Some scholars suggest that around 500 people were present. However, in chapter two, when the Holy Spirit descended, only 120 were gathered in the upper room, waiting. The remaining 380 may have been preoccupied, fatigued, or occupied with other tasks. Regardless of the reason, they missed out on experiencing what God had promised.

Those 120 in the upper room were united in purpose. The Bible says, "*. . . they were all together in one place. Suddenly a sound like the blowing of a violent wind came from heaven and filled the whole house . . .* " (Acts 2:1-2, NIV). When you are connected with other Believers in the house of God, together in unity, you are in a position to receive something special from Heaven.

I read about redwood trees in California, the tallest trees in the world, which can grow over 350 feet in height and live for more than two thousand years. They're incredibly resilient, withstanding winds, storms, pests, and all kinds of things that would cause other trees to fall. What's interesting is that the redwood's roots reach down in the ground less than twelve feet, with the biggest root being one inch in diameter. How can those small roots, only a fraction of the height of the tree, keep the tree up? What's unique about their roots is that they are intertwined with other redwoods. They grow close to each other, but their roots spread out a hundred feet and connect with all the other redwoods close by. When the winds blow, even though it can be a powerful storm, the redwood tree doesn't just rely on its roots but the roots of many trees around them, causing the entire forest to be linked together. That wind is not blowing against one tree; it's blowing against thousands of trees. That's how the redwood tree can stand thousands of years. Each one has the root strength of the whole forest.

Let us think of ways to motivate one another to acts of love and good works. And let us not neglect our meeting together, as some people do, but encourage one another, especially now that the day of his return is drawing near.
Hebrews 10:24–25 (NLT)

You were not meant to journey through life alone. You were designed to be connected, to be a part of a family of

faith. When you're firmly planted in the house of the Lord, your roots get connected with mine and others, creating a support system that makes you unshakeable. We're there to stabilize you, steady you, and encourage you. And scripture says that "one can chase a thousand, but two can put ten thousand to flight" (see Deuteronomy 32:30). Imagine the power when we're all connected. No weapon formed against us can prosper. Together, we are more resilient, stronger, and unbeatable.

When you're planted in the house of the Lord, you'll not only see breakthroughs happen, but your faith will create an atmosphere for God to bless others too. We are better together!

Be Encouraged Today:

When we are gathered together as one, with one purpose, and everyone present is seeking God, there is an opportunity for the Holy Spirit to move among us, and miraculous things can happen.

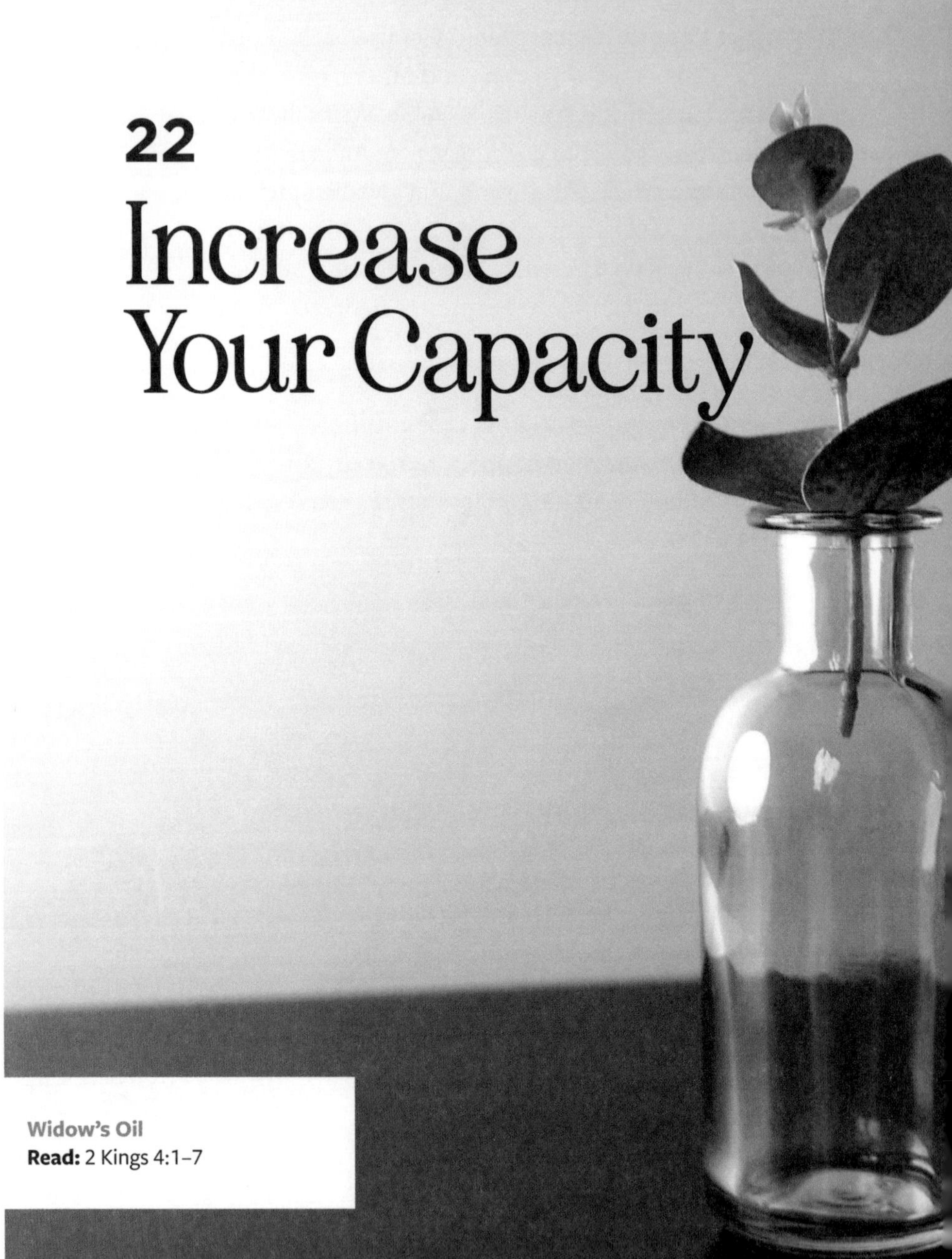

22
Increase Your Capacity

Widow's Oil
Read: 2 Kings 4:1–7

In 2 Kings, there's the story of a widow whose husband had died, leaving her in debt and with creditors threatening to take her sons as slaves for payment. All she had left of any value was a small jar of oil. She asked help from Elisha the prophet, who instructed her to borrow as many empty containers from her neighbors as she could. He specifically said, "Not just a few."

She and her sons gathered maybe a dozen containers and returned. Elisha instructed her to pour the little oil she had into one of the empty containers. It didn't make sense; however, she did it anyway. Miraculously, she filled up the first container, then another, and another, until she had filled all the containers she had gathered. The oil never ran out until she ran out of containers. She sold the oil, as Elisha had instructed, and had enough to pay her debts and plenty left to live on.

The key phrase in this story is "borrow not a few." The widow determined how much oil she was going to have. The oil ran out when she didn't have any more containers. That's why God told her, "Borrow not just a few." If she had borrowed twice as many containers, she would have had twice as much oil. What if she had said, "Elisha, I've got this cup; let's just use it."? She would have only had a cup full of oil.

For it was I, the LORD your God, who rescued you from the land of Egypt. Open your mouth wide, and I will fill it with good things.
Psalm 81:10 (NLT)

God is showing us a principle: If you increase your capacity to receive, He will fill it. His supply is unlimited and never runs out. However, too often, due to disappointments and delays, we have watered down our dreams and lowered our expectations. We are not stretching or believing for great things but settling for just a few containers. God has the oil, but we often lack the capacity to receive it. He is saying to you what He said to this woman, "Borrow not a few."

Don't shortchange yourself by living with a limited mentality. *I'll never get out of debt. God, just help me pay my bills and help us to get along. No, pray bold prayers!* God is ready to fill the containers you bring to Him. It's not a supply problem;

it's a capacity problem. Increase your capacity to receive and don't put limits on what God wants to do in your life? Are you focused only on what you think can happen within your ability? God controls the universe and is supernatural and all-powerful. Don't base your container capacity on what you can do; base your capacity on what God can do.

Be Encouraged Today:

Don't live with a limited mentality of what is possible. Increase your capacity to receive, and God, who has an unlimited supply, will fill all the containers you bring to Him.

23
Your Yes Is Coming

Hezekiah's Healing
Read: 2 Kings 20:7

In 2 Kings 20, Hezekiah was very sick, nearing death. He desired God to heal him, but God told him no. Then, the prophet Isaiah, Hezekiah's mentor, showed up at the palace. I can imagine that when Hezekiah heard the news that Isaiah was there, he cheered up, thinking, *Maybe there's hope. Perhaps he'll pray for me, and I'll get well. Or maybe he'll give me an encouraging word that I can stand on.*

Isaiah came in and said, "Hezekiah, I have a word from the Lord for you." Hezekiah leaned in closer. Isaiah said, "The Lord says, 'Set your house in order, you will surely die.'" He didn't say, "You might die," or "It doesn't look too good, Hezekiah," or "There's a small chance you may pull through." He said, "You will surely die." It was a strong statement. "There is no doubt, it is certain, you will die."

What do you do when God says no? Hezekiah could have thought, *Well, I guess that's it. I'm done. There's no use in even trying.* But the scripture says Hezekiah turned his face to the wall and began to pray. He reminded God how he had served Him, how he had torn down the pagan altars, how he hadn't followed in the footsteps of his father, and how he had set a new standard for his family. He asked God for His mercy, to give him more years. His attitude was, "If I die, I'm going to die believing for a yes." Before Isaiah left the palace grounds, God said to him, "Go back and tell Hezekiah I have heard his prayer, and I've changed my mind. I'm going to say yes and heal him and add fifteen years to his life."

Whatever God has promised gets stamped with the Yes of Jesus. In him, this is what we preach and pray, the great Amen, God's Yes and our Yes together, gloriously evident. God affirms us, making us a sure thing in Christ, putting his Yes within us. By his Spirit, He has stamped us with his eternal pledge — a sure beginning of what he is destined to complete.
2 Corinthians 1:20 (MSG)

Even when you feel like God has said no, if you do like Hezekiah and dare to ask for the yes, your faith can cause God to change your course. Mistakes that you've made, God's going to give you another chance. Opportunities that you've missed, they're going to come back across your path. Things that have been a struggle, they're going to suddenly turn around.

Paul said in 2 Corinthians 1:20–21, *"Whatever God has promised gets stamped with Yes of Jesus"* (MSG). It's already on the schedule, but there's one thing God needs. It goes on to say, *"God's yes and our yes together, makes a sure thing."* God works where there's faith. God's yes by itself is not enough; now He wants your yes to make it happen.

Have you let the nos, the disappointments, the delays convince you that it's never going to happen. You may not have seen it yet, but this is a new day. You're coming into your year of yes. Now add your yes to God's yes.

Be Encouraged Today:

God works where there's faith. God wants your yes to make it happen. He is always ready to bless and advance you.

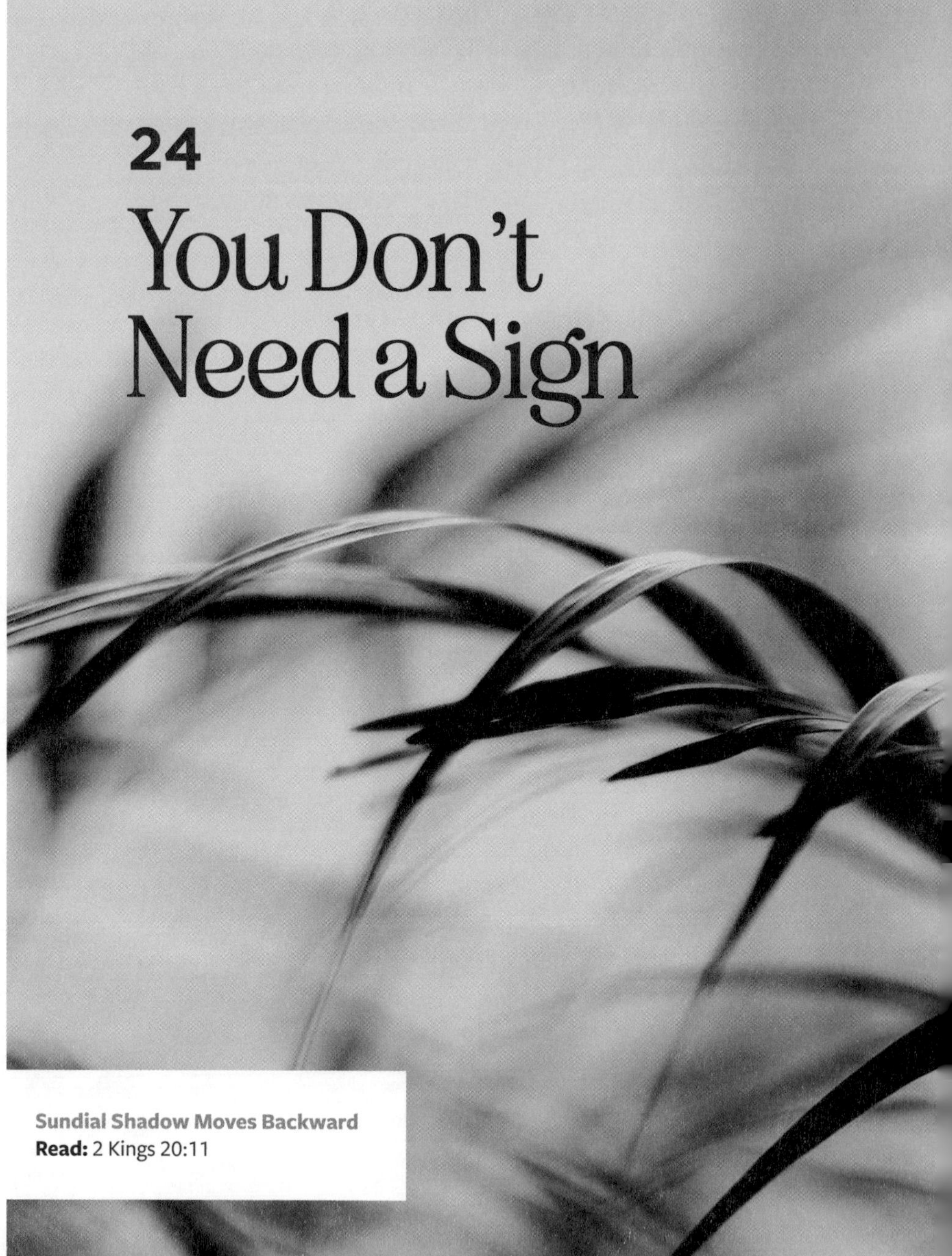

24
You Don't Need a Sign

Sundial Shadow Moves Backward
Read: 2 Kings 20:11

When Hezekiah poured out his heart and asked God to spare his life, 2 Kings 20:5–6 says, "*I have heard your prayer and seen your tears. I will heal you, and three days from now you will get out of bed ... I will add fifteen more years to your life*" (NLT). You can imagine how excited and how overwhelmed Hezekiah was. He just received this amazing promise that this death sentence had been reversed.

After the excitement wore off, Hezekiah started thinking, *How do I know I'm going to get well? I don't look any different, I don't feel any better, nothing has changed. Doubt started to set in. Is it really going to happen?* In 2 Kings 20:8, Hezekiah said to Isaiah, "*What will be the sign that the LORD will heal me...*" (NIV). He meant, "Isaiah,

I appreciate what you've told me; that's encouraging, but I'm going to need some evidence. I need to see something, so I can believe that it is true. I need God to prove that He's going to do it."

Faith shows the reality of what we hope for; it is the evidence of things we cannot see.
Hebrews 11:1 (NLT)

Isaiah said, "Alright, God will give you a sign. Do you want the shadow on the sundial to go forward ten steps or backward ten steps?" Hezekiah said 'backward.' They watched as the shadow defied nature and went backward. Not only a sign but a true miracle.

God is merciful, and sometimes He will give you a sign. However, if you live by this approach, "God, prove that You're going to do what You said. God, I need some evidence. If I don't see something then I'm not going to believe." If you're always dependent on a sign, you won't reach the fullness of your destiny. The miracles in your life will be greatly limited. Maybe like Hezekiah, you're praying for a sign, but you're not seeing anything.

It's great to receive a sign, but don't rely on it. Don't become dependent on seeing before you believe. That doesn't require faith. Your faith is demonstrated when there is no

evidence. The Bible says, "*Faith shows the reality of what we hope for; it is the evidence of things we cannot see*" (Hebrews 11:1, NLT).

The right attitude is: God, I don't have to have a sign. I don't have to see it to believe it. You've already proved to me who You are. God, I trust You without evidence. I'm not like Hezekiah, needing You to prove Your faithfulness. You have already shown Yourself faithful.

Be Encouraged Today:

Instead of asking God to prove to you what He's going to do, turn it around and show God who you are — a man or woman of faith. Prove to Him that you won't be moved by what you don't see. Your faith in Him and His promises are all the evidence you need to receive your miracle.

25

God Will Complete Your Incompleteness

Man Raised from the Dead

Read: 2 Kings 13:21

The prophet Elisha was promised a double portion of Elijah's anointing. The Bible records seven major miracles attributed to Elijah, but when Elisha was lying on his deathbed, he had only performed thirteen major miracles, one short of the double anointing he was promised. However, God is a God of completion and knows how to fulfill His promises.

Later, when Elisha died without performing that final miracle, it seemed like his promise was unfulfilled and incomplete, but remember, it's not over until God says it's over. When Elisha died, they buried him in an open grave. I can imagine them chiseling on his tombstone, 'He almost had a double portion and almost fulfilled his destiny. However, he was one miracle short.'

Around that time, a man had died, and those burying him saw a gang of robbers coming. They hastily threw the body into Elisha's open grave. When the body touched Elisha's bones, the dead man came back to life, stood up, and walked out of the grave.

And I am certain that God, who began the good work within you, will continue his work until it is finally finished on the day when Christ Jesus returns.
Philippians 1:6 (NLT)

I can imagine those burying him took off running. That was miracle number fourteen, the final one Elisha was promised. This story teaches us that, as long as we stay in faith, as long as we keep believing, every promise God has made will come to pass. Not even death can prevent God from fulfilling His promises.

We all have things that we would consider to be incompletions, a dream in our heart unfulfilled. You had promises you were standing on, but you faced obstacles. Now time has passed, and you've given up. Deep down, you know the promise is incomplete. Today, I urge you to recalibrate your vision. Don't just see it as it is now; see it completed and fulfilled. The Bible says that "He who has begun a good work in you will complete it" (see Philippians 1:6).

When you're tempted to get discouraged, turn it around. Say, "Father, I want to thank You that You will finish what You started in my life. I know You are a God of completion." Remember, it's not by our might or power, but God's power and favor. If you're determined to go out each day in faith and expectancy and hold fast to what God has promised, He will complete your incompletions. Not even death can keep God from bringing it to completion.

Be Encouraged Today:

God is the Author and the Finisher of your faith. Every promise, dream, and desire God's given you will come to pass. If you will hold fast to what God's put in your heart, stay in faith, and keep your hopes up, God will complete your incompletions.

26

Stay Open to God's Way

Jesus Walks on Water
Read: Matthew 14:22–33

One evening, the disciples were in a boat on the Sea of Galilee. They were rowing across the lake in the middle of the night when a strong wind began to blow against them. It was almost impossible to keep moving forward and get to the other side. As they struggled and struggled, I can hear them say, "I wish Jesus was here with us. He could calm these winds down. If He was here, it would be so much easier."

Suddenly, Jesus came walking on the water toward the boat. One translation says, "*They were terrified and started screaming.*" They thought it was a ghost. What happened? Jesus showed up in a different way than they expected, and they didn't recognize Him. They had never seen Him in that form, and certainly not walking on the surface of the water.

For just as the heavens are higher than the earth, so my ways are higher than your ways and my thoughts higher than your thoughts.
Isaiah 55:9 (NLT)

They had seen Him during the day, teaching on the Sea of Galilee. They had seen Him feeding the 5,000 and healing the lepers. They knew what He looked like during the daytime. But they'd never seen Him in the middle of the night during a great storm walking on the water. Sometimes, when God shows up in an unexpected way, we don't recognize Him.

God could be sending your answer right now. Jesus could be walking on the water right beside your boat. But because the answer is not what you thought it would look like, because you have preconceived ideas, this may keep you from seeing what God is showing you. My challenge to you is to stay open to all possibilities. The answer may not come in a familiar way. It may not happen like it did last time. God may show up in an unexpected form.

God used Pharaoh's daughter to take care of baby Moses. In other words, God used the enemy to take care of His

children. Friend, God is God. He can do what He wants to do. Don't put God in a box and miss your miracle, because He may show up in a way you least expect.

My challenge to you is to stay open. Don't be set in your thinking to where it can only happen one way, and you've told God how to do it, who to use, and when it could happen. Let God out of your box. He may not use somebody that's on your "approved to use" list.

Be Encouraged Today:

The way God does things is not how we do them. His ways are better and higher than our limited ways. And if you will stay open and let God do it His way, you'll see your miracle.

27
Your Gifts Will Return

Cornelius' Vision
Read: Acts 10:3–4, 30–32

In Acts 10, there's a story about a Roman army captain named Cornelius. The Bible describes him as a good man who prayed often and gave generously to the poor. One translation even calls him "a generous giver." The chapter tells how he had a vision, an angel appeared to him, and he eventually connected with Peter.

Cornelius and his family were the first Gentile household chosen to receive the good news and salvation after Jesus' resurrection. Why do you think God chose him? Scripture gives us insight in verse 4, where the angel tells Cornelius, *"Your prayers and your generous gifts to the poor have come up as a memorial before God"* (NIV). One translation says, *"Your prayers and charities have not gone unnoticed by God"* (TLB).

Don't let anyone convince you that giving doesn't make a difference. Cornelius was chosen because of his giving attitude. The scripture says that "his prayers not only went up to God, but his generous gifts went up as well." Likewise, when we give, it gets God's attention in a special way. God sees your gifts, and every time you help somebody, He sees your acts of kindness. Like Cornelius, it gets God's attention, and He'll begin to pour out His favor in a new way in your life.

Send your grain across the seas, and in time, profits will flow back to you.
Ecclesiastes 11:1 (NLT)

In your time of need, learn to do more than pray. Learn to sow a seed. Put some action behind your prayers. It's one thing to pray, "God, help my child get back on course." That is great, but if you really want to get God's attention, after you pray, go help somebody else's child get back on course. When you're generous with others, God will always be generous with you. And if you'll stop thinking about how you can be blessed and start thinking of ways you can be a blessing, then God will meet all your needs in abundance.

Do like Cornelius and do something to help others. Your gifts will go up as a memorial before God. Maybe you're

believing for something that means a lot to you. I encourage you to sow a special seed for that specific need. Your gifts don't go unnoticed by God. Giving gets His attention. I'm not saying that we can buy a miracle or God's goodness, but we can, just like Cornelius, exercise our faith through our giving. And if you want to see God's favor in a new way, do more than pray. Be a generous giver.

Be Encouraged Today:

God sees your gifts and acts of kindness. By being a generous giver, you'll get God's attention, and you'll see His favor in a new way. Put your faith into action and live that life of victory that God has in store for you.

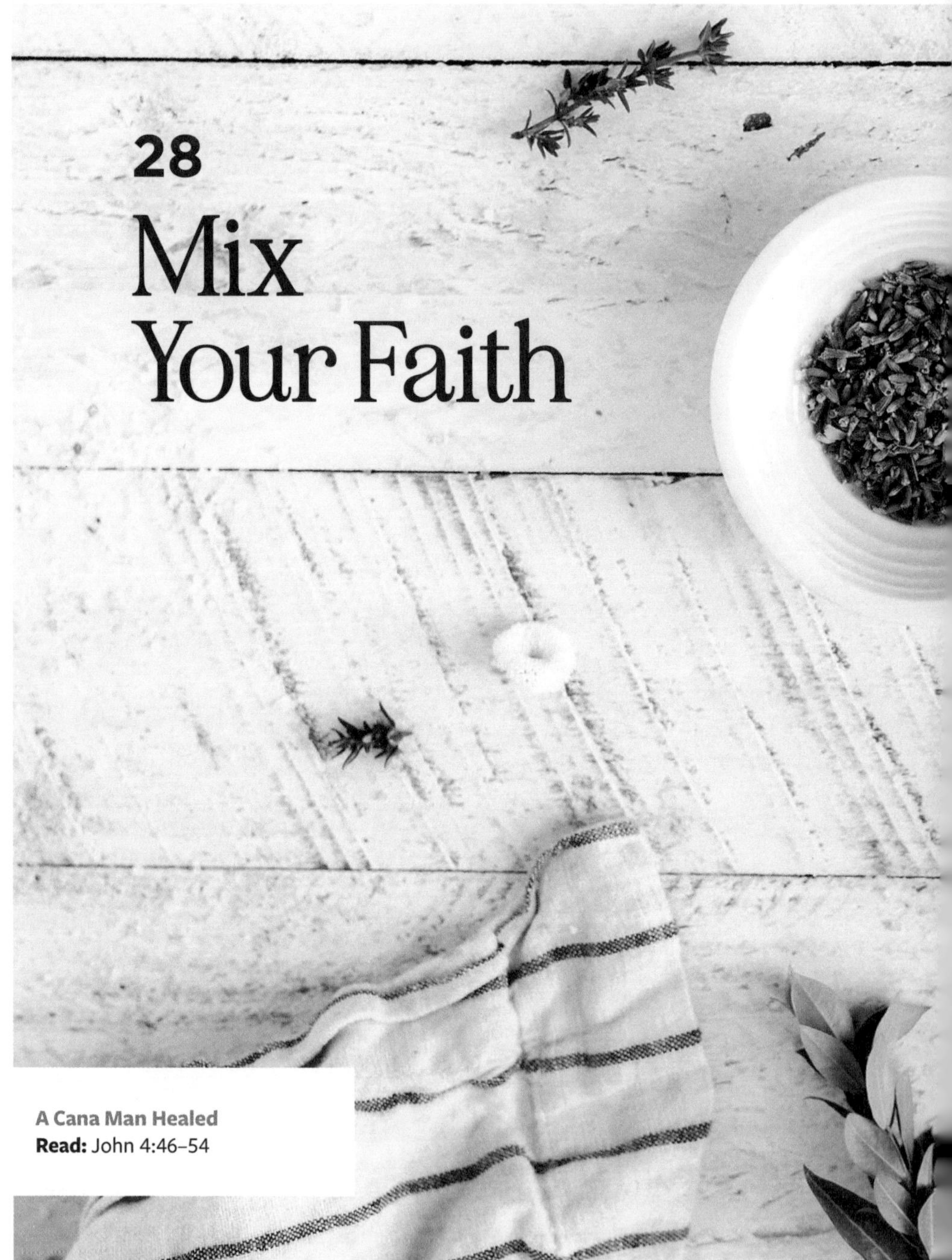

28

Mix Your Faith

A Cana Man Healed
Read: John 4:46–54

In John 4, Jesus was traveling through the region of Galilee and came to the town of Cana. There was a government official in another city who had a son that was very sick, close to death. When he heard Jesus was in Cana, he hurried over, fell at Jesus' feet, and begged Him to heal his son. Jesus didn't go at first, but the man pleaded and said, "Please, Jesus, come now, my little boy is about to die." Jesus looked at the man and said, "You can go back home. Your son is healed!"

The man believed Jesus' word and started back home. This man could have thought, *I'm not leaving. Jesus, you didn't even pray for my son. I'm staying here until you come with me.* No, his attitude was, I have heard the promise from Jesus, that my son is well. I'm not going to entertain any doubt; I'll only add the right ingredient: my faith. He turned around and headed home.

...but word which they heard did not profit them, not being mixed with faith in those who heard it.
Hebrews 4:2 (NKJV)

All he had was a promise. But he did what I'm asking us to do: he mixed faith with it. He wasn't moved by circumstances. He wasn't discouraged because Jesus didn't come. He just kept thanking God for what he heard. Every thought told him, *Jesus wouldn't come. It's too late.* He had a thousand reasons to doubt, to worry, to be upset, but he just kept mixing his faith with the promise. *I believe what Jesus said, that my son will live.*

While he was walking home with the expectation of a miracle, people from his house came running toward him. I can imagine him seeing them in the distance, thoughts could have started bombarding his mind, *They're coming with bad news. Your son didn't make it. It's too late.* Deep down, he kept playing those words, "Thank you, Jesus. I believe what You said that my son will live." The people finally made it to him. They smiled and said, "We have good news. Suddenly, your son got better for no apparent reason. Now he's perfectly

well, running around, playing like nothing was ever wrong." This is what happens when you mix the right ingredient — faith — with God's promises. Dare to believe what God has told you. You're closer than you think. This is not the time to start doubting. Now more than ever, you need to stir up your faith and mix it into your situation.

Be Encouraged Today:

Keep declaring what God has promised. Keep talking like it's on the way. Keep mixing in your faith because that's what activates God's power to bring His promises to life.

29
Stretch Out

A Withered Hand is Healed
Read: Matthew 12:10–13

There is a story in the New Testament about a man who is simply called "the man with the withered hand." When Jesus went into the Capernaum synagogue, He noticed the man. The Pharisees were there as well, hoping to find Jesus breaking the law so they could charge Him.

Jesus said to the man, "Stretch out your hand." And he stretched it out, it was restored as whole as the other. That withered hand represents how life can wear us down.

When something withers, it's a gradual process; it doesn't happen overnight. When Victoria and I have been given flowers, we take them home and put them in a vase on our kitchen table. They are very beautiful and vivid with color, a picture of a perfect life. After a week or two, little by little, they start to wither. It's such a slow process; you can barely tell their color and vibrancy are slowly getting duller. But after a few weeks, it is very clear they're totally withered.

He lifted me out of the pit of despair, out of the mud and the mire. He set my feet on solid ground and steadied me as I walked along. He has given me a new song to sing, a hymn of praise to our God. Many will see what he has done and be amazed. They will put their trust in the LORD.
Psalm 40:2–3 (NLT)

If we're not careful, that's what can happen to us in life. We start out passionate about our dreams. We're going to do something great in life. But then we hit some setbacks. We don't realize it, but little by little, life has withered us, and we have lost our passion.

It's interesting Jesus didn't say to the man, "Sir, I'm sorry that you have a withered hand, and you can't do what other people can do." No, Jesus asked him to do something the man had never done before, which could seem cruel. He looked at him and said, "Sir, stretch out your hand." The man had to decide in that moment if he could do what he had never done before.

The man could have made excuses. "Jesus, I can't stretch out my hand. I was born this way." He did not make any excuses. He dared to take a step of faith and stretched out his hand. The Scripture says, *"Immediately he was made whole."*

Life may have withered you in some area along the way; you got discouraged and now you've given up on your dream. God is saying to us what He said to this man, "Stretch out your hand." Stretch out what is withered. Stretch your mind to think in a new way. Stretch your vision and stretch your faith.

Will you, in faith, stretch out what is withered and seems to be dying in your life and do what you thought you could never do?

Be Encouraged Today:

God has a way of rejuvenating and restoring what looks withered or dead. He is the Glory and the Lifter of our heads. Let Him lift your head. Stretch out your neck and look up from where you are, getting a fresh vision, and see what is possible. He will set your feet on a rock and put a new song in your heart. You'll soar through life full of joy, full of faith, full of victory.

30
Your Turnaround Is Coming

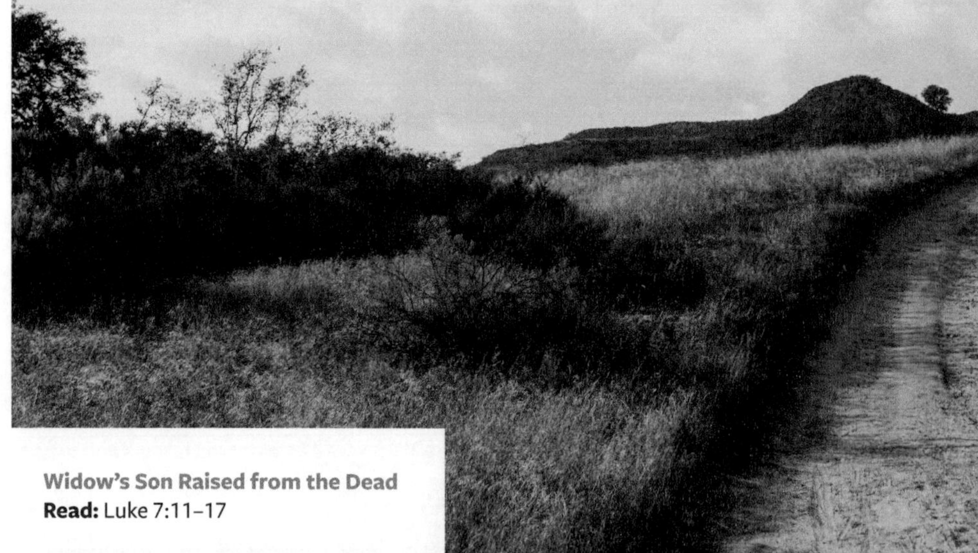

Widow's Son Raised from the Dead
Read: Luke 7:11–17

In Luke 7, Jesus had left Capernaum and headed to the city of Nain. His disciples and a large group of people were following him. When he arrived at the city, a funeral procession was coming toward Him on their way to bury a young boy. His mother was a widow and had already buried her husband, and now she was about to bury her only son. You can imagine the sorrow, the pain she was dealing with.

In those days, her son represented her security; that's how she would be taken care of. Now her support for her latter years was gone. The Bible says, *"When Jesus saw her, his heart broke"* (Luke 7:13, MSG). God sees when you're hurting. He sees when you're lonely, when you feel overwhelmed, and you can't go on. Jesus is moved with compassion.

Jesus went over to the woman and said, "Don't cry." His heart went out to her and He was encouraging her not to cry because He was about to turn things around. He knew this pain and sorrow would not be permanent and that this was not how her story would end. He walked over to the coffin. The pallbearers set it down. Jesus spoke to the little boy and said, "Young man, wake up." The little boy sat up in the coffin and began to look around. Jesus went over, picked him up, and handed him to his mother, alive and well.

You have turned my mourning into joyful dancing. You have taken away my clothes of mourning and clothed me with joy.
Psalm 30:11 (NLT)

This widow went from great sorrow to great joy, from great mourning to great rejoicing. She was depressed and distraught, not knowing how she could go on, but then the God of the turnaround stepped in. Now her tears are no longer tears of sadness, but tears of joy.

Sometimes life gets tough. You shed tears from hurts, something that breaks your heart. There are times of mourning in our lives, but that's not the end because the God of the turnaround has not stepped in. As with this woman, He's going to step in and turn that sorrow to joy, turn that brokenness to wholeness, turn that mourning into dancing.

This miracle teaches us to see Him as a turnaround God. Imagine a funeral procession interrupted by Jesus, who raises the boy to life. They don't proceed to the burial plot but return to the city, astonished by the unexpected turnaround in their favor. When people ask why they are back so soon, they say, "We had a turnaround."

We all have situations that look dead, but God is saying, "I'm going to bring dead things back to life." There are going to be turnarounds that leave you in awe. You left defeated but you're going to come back victorious. Increase is coming, favor is coming, new clients are coming. A turnaround is coming. God is about to do something out of the ordinary, something supernatural. Like the people in this miracle, you're going to be in awe, amazed at the goodness of God.

Be Encouraged Today:

God is a turnaround God. What seemed lifeless can be revitalized; what seemed fractured can be restored. God can transform your hardships into moments of ease and your mourning into joy, leading to a life filled with blessings and contentment.

What God put in your heart is en route. You are close to your miracle.

- JOEL

Cured of Cancer

On December 11, 1981, my mother and father prayed and asked God to heal her from cancer and give her more years with us. My mother believed that day that she received her healing. She went from night to day, but nothing looked any different. She was still very frail, her skin was still yellow, and she only weighed eighty-nine pounds, but I never heard her complain; she never talked defeat. She would go through the house, quoting Scripture, "I will live and not die, and declare the works of the Lord." It was still dark; the medical report hadn't changed. Month after month, there were no signs of improvement.

All of her senses said, It's not going to work out. She didn't look good, and she didn't feel well. Her emotions and her thoughts said she wasn't going to make it, but she wasn't moved by that. She kept thanking God, walking by faith and not by sight. Sight said, "It's dark; nothing has changed. You'll never get well." But faith said, "I've entered a new day. It's dark now, but light is coming. It's just a matter of time before healing breaks through the horizon." It didn't happen suddenly like Paul and Silas, but over time, little by little, she started getting better and better. Her skin color came back to normal, she gained her weight back, and she gained strength. Today, more than forty years later, she's perfectly healthy and whole. No cancer in her body. Remember: God has the final say over sickness.

"She kept thanking God, walking by faith and not by sight."

modern-day miracles

Mailroom Miracle

My sister Lisa was born with a condition like cerebral palsy. The doctors told my parents she would probably never be able to walk or feed herself. The first year, she couldn't lift her head and had no sucking reflexes. By the grace of God, she got better and defied the odds. Growing up, there were five of us kids; all of us except Lisa were very athletic and played sports. Lisa, having come through this birth condition, couldn't do everything we did. When we were choosing teams with our friends to play kickball at the house, she would always be chosen at the very end. It seemed like it was one thing after another for Lisa. In her early twenties, she went through a breakup in a relationship that was very hurtful and not fair.

In 1990, she was working at the church, opening my father's mail. She opened this package, and it exploded in her lap. It was a mail bomb. It blew up part of her leg and injured her stomach. She was rushed to the hospital and had to have surgery. The investigators said if the package had been turned longways in her lap instead of sideways, it would have killed her instantly. It was a pipe bomb; the nails shot out the side, away from her instead of into her. Why did she have all these things coming against her since she was a little baby? The enemy knew there was something special inside her — an anointing to teach, a gift to lead, a favor to help build people. Every time the enemy tried to stop her, God stepped up and said, "Peace. Be still." When the bomb exploded, God said, "Bomb, you can't finish her off. I have the final say." God refused to let her enemies triumph. Lisa says, "I opened the bomb, but now I am the bomb." Like Lisa, take courage in the truth that your destiny cannot be stopped by the plans of the enemy. God has the final word.

"Every time the enemy tried to stop her, God stepped up."

Securing the Compaq Center

A few years after I started ministering, the church began to grow. I thought we would build a new auditorium. That's the way I had seen my father do it growing up. He had built sanctuary after sanctuary. We found some property right off the freeway, by the other location. It seemed perfect to me, but when we went to close on it, the owner sold it out from under us. He didn't keep his word. I was disappointed. I knew that property was supposed to be ours. We found another hundred-acre tract not far away, and the same thing happened. I couldn't understand why those doors kept closing. There were no more large tracts of land to build on by the other location. My father always said that he would never move the church. My mind wasn't open for the new thing God had in store. About six months later, the Compaq Center came available. I never dreamed we could have this building. This was so much bigger and better than I ever imagined. It was a three-year battle, but we saw the hand of God make rivers in the desert, move giants out of the way, and bring the right people to help us.

We had a consultant who was very influential and knew all the inner workings of the city. He had never been to church, didn't have anything to do with God or faith. He partied, used bad language, cursed people out. But he said, "Joel, I like you, and I'm going to help you get this building." God has already lined up the people you need for the new thing. Stay open. It may not happen the way you're expecting, but can I encourage you? God's way will be better, bigger, more rewarding, more fulfilling. Don't limit what God is going to do in your future to what you've seen in the past. God never does His greatest feats in your yesterdays; they are always in your tomorrows.

"God's way will be better, bigger, more rewarding, and more fulfilling."

modern-day miracles

Medical Missions Vision

At twelve years old, my brother Paul had a dream to do medical missions. He was on a trip to Africa with my father. Standing on a hot tarmac, waiting for a plane to refuel in a small area called Northern Rhodesia, he felt a desire to come back and help the people. Paul went on to medical school and started his practice as a surgeon in Arkansas. He was very successful, the chief of surgery, helping to run the hospital. He tried several times to take missions trips, but it didn't work out. He had too much responsibility. When my father went to be with the Lord in 1999, Paul left his medical practice after nearly twenty years and came back home to help us pastor the church. He thought his dream of doing medical missions was over. But years later, long after he had been out of medicine, a friend called and asked if he would go overseas with a group of doctors just to see what they did. He finally agreed to go. While he was there, they put him in the operating room and said, "We need you to operate on these people." He said, "I haven't operated in years. I didn't sign up for this; I came to observe." They said, "We need you now." Paul unexpectedly came out of retirement that day and started operating again.

My brother thought his dream was over. He thought he'd stepped out of medicine. But just because you gave up doesn't mean God gave up. Now Paul spends about five months a year in Africa, operating in the remote villages where they barely have electricity. Not long ago, when he was in Zambia, he saw an old book with the words "Northern Rhodesia" stamped on the inside cover, and he realized that Zambia used to be called Northern Rhodesia. He was at the exact place where that dream was planted in his heart over forty years earlier as a twelve-year-old boy. At twelve years old (that was the first touch), God gave him the dream; at fifty-six years old (that was the second touch), God thrust him into the fullness of his destiny. God will finish the good work He has started in your life.

"Just because you gave up doesn't mean God gave up."

modern-day miracles

Surgical Equipment Miracle

My brother Paul was in Haiti right after the big earthquake. He and a team of surgeons were operating on all the injured people. They were at a hospital about twenty miles outside of Port-au-Prince. One day, the main monitor they were using during surgery to monitor the patients' blood pressure and heart rate went out. Without that monitor, they couldn't do any more surgeries. They told the man in charge, and he started searching all over the small hospital, but they didn't have another one. Paul and the team started making phone calls and doing everything they could to get word out, but with no success. It was very frustrating to have the ability and skill and talent, but not having one small thing was keeping them from helping so many people. It looked like it would be several days before they could get one flown in.

A few hours later, the hospital administrator, a local Haitian man, came in carrying a brand-new monitor, still in the box. Paul and the other surgeons were amazed that he would have the exact monitor that they needed. Paul asked him where he got it. He told how two years earlier he was at a hospital administrator's conference in America. Everyone that attended was entered into a contest for a door prize. Out of several thousand people, it just so happened that he won this monitor. He had no use for it at the time. It was in storage. But God knows what you're going to need in the future. He knows who you're going to need. The good news is He's going ahead of you. He's lining up the right breaks, the right people, the right opportunities. He has solutions to problems you haven't even had. Before you call, He's going to answer you.

"God knows what you're going to need in the future."

What He has purposed for your life will come to pass. No matter your circumstances, trust His timing and trust His ways. There's a miracle about to take place.

- JOEL

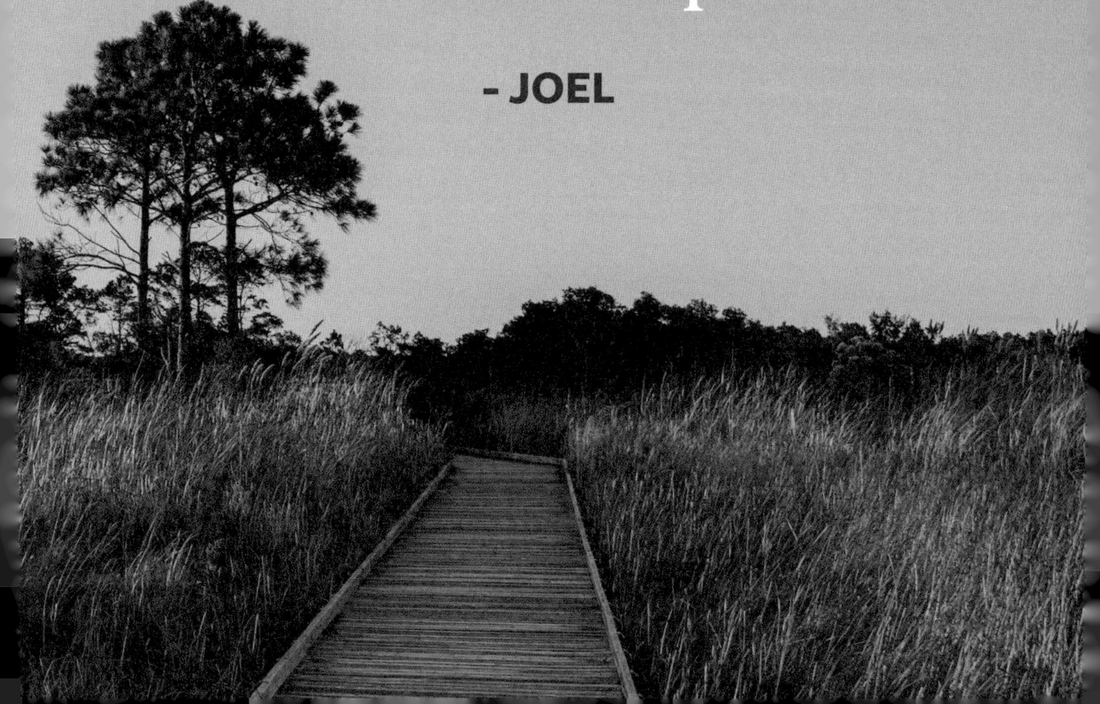

Old Testament Miracles

1. **The Creation of Heaven and Earth and All Living Creatures – Genesis 1:1–27.** The Bible describes the account of how God created the heavens and the earth in six days – forming light, sky, land, seas, vegetation, celestial bodies, sea creatures, animals, and ultimately, humankind, culminating in the creation of man and woman in His image.

2. **The Great Flood – Genesis 7:17–24.** God sends rain upon the earth for forty days and forty nights, causing the waters to rise and cover the entire earth, destroying all living creatures except those aboard Noah's ark.

3. **Confusion of Tongues at Babel – Genesis 11:3–9.** The story of the Tower of Babel, where humanity's attempt to build a tower to reach the heavens results in God confusing their language, leading to the dispersion of people across the earth with many languages.

4. **Angels Guarded Lot – Genesis 19:10–11.** This story tells of angels guarding Lot's household in Sodom from the hostile intentions of the city's men, showing God's protection and intervention in times of perversion and peril.

5. **Cities of Sodom and Gomorrah Destroyed – Genesis 19:24–25.** This was a cataclysmic miracle where fire and brimstone rained down from the sky, obliterating the cities and their inhabitants. The destruction of Sodom and Gomorrah is often cited as a warning against the consequences of sin and disobedience to God.

6. **Lot's Wife Turned to a Pillar of Salt – Genesis 19:26.** This event recounts the tragic fate of Lot's wife, who, against divine instruction, looks back at the destruction of Sodom and Gomorrah and is consequently transformed into a pillar of salt.

7. **Donkey Speaks in Human Voice – Numbers 22:21–35.** This miracle is a story of Balaam's donkey speaking like a human, preventing Balaam from continuing a misguided path.

8. **Burning Bush – Exodus 3:3.** This miraculous event occurs when Moses encounters a burning bush that is not consumed by the flames, letting him know he is in God's presence, and God speaks to him from within the bush.

9. **Moses' Rod Changes into a Serpent – Exodus 4:3–4, 30.** God miraculously transforms Moses' rod into a snake, revealing to Pharoah that God's power and authority is with Moses as he prepares to lead the Israelites out of Egypt.

10. **Moses' Hand Made Leprous – Exodus 4:6–7, 30.** God demonstrates His power by making Moses' hand leprous and then healing it instantly.

11. **Aaron's Rod Changes into a Serpent – Exodus 7:8–10.** Aaron's rod is miraculously transformed into a serpent before Pharaoh and his magicians, displaying God's power and authority as He communicates His will through Moses and Aaron during the confrontation with Egypt's ruler.

12. **Nile River Turned to Blood – Exodus 7:20–25.** God demonstrates His supremacy over Egypt's gods by turning the Nile River into blood. This act is a sign of God's judgment and power, setting the stage for the liberation of the Israelites from slavery.

13. **The Plague of Frogs – Exodus 8:1–15.** Egypt is plagued by a multitude of frogs, a miraculous event revealing God's authority and His power over the natural world, compelling Pharaoh to acknowledge God's command through Moses.

14. **The Plague of Gnats – Exodus 8:16–19.** Egypt is overcome by swarms of gnats, a miraculous event that demonstrates God's control over creation and

serves as a sign of His judgment, compelling Pharaoh to recognize God's supremacy.

15. **The Plague of Flies – Exodus 8:20–24.** Egypt is overwhelmed by a plague of flies, showcasing God's power and authority as He continues to confront Pharaoh through miraculous signs, compelling him to release the Israelites from bondage.

16. **The Plague of Murrain – Exodus 9:1–7.** Egypt is struck by a severe murrain, a high fever and inflammation, affecting its livestock. This is seen as God's judgment as He enforces His will through Moses, further pressuring Pharaoh to let the Israelites go.

17. **The Plague of Boils – Exodus 9:8–12.** Egyptians are afflicted with painful boils, a warning to Pharaoh to heed His commands through Moses, yet Pharaoh's heart remains hardened.

18. **The Plague of Hail – Exodus 9:18–24.** A severe hailstorm of unprecedented ferocity devastates Egypt. Through His power, God protects the Israelites while bringing devastation upon the land, compelling Pharaoh to acknowledge God's supremacy.

19. **The Plague of Locusts – Exodus 10:1–20.** Egypt is overrun by a massive swarm of locusts, displaying God's authority and control over nature as He continues to challenge Pharaoh through miraculous signs, urging him to release the Israelites.

20. **The Plague of Darkness – Exodus 10:21–23.** Complete darkness covers all of Egypt for three days, except where the people of Israel lived.

21. **The Plague of the Firstborn – Exodus 12:29–30.** The final plague strikes Egypt as the firstborn in every household, including livestock, dies by God's judgment. A pivotal moment in the Israelites' journey towards liberation as Pharaoh finally relents and allows them to leave.

22. **The Pillar of Cloud and Fire – Exodus 13:21–22; 14:19–20.** The miraculous pillar of cloud by day and fire by night guides and protects the Israelites during their escape from Egypt, demonstrating God's continuous presence and guidance as they journey toward freedom.

23. **The Crossing of the Red Sea – Exodus 14:21–23.** God parts the Red Sea, allowing the Israelites to cross on dry land and escape the pursuing Egyptian army, killing Pharoah and delivering His people from imminent danger.

24. **Bitter Waters Sweetened – Exodus 15:25.** At Marah, God miraculously sweetened bitter waters to make them drinkable because He cared for the needs of the Israelites and His ability to transform difficulties into blessings.

25. **Manna from Heaven – Exodus 16:13–36.** God provides manna to sustain the Israelites during their journey in the wilderness, demonstrating that He is the source of their provision and emphasizing His faithfulness to His people.

26. **Water From the Rock at Rephidim – Exodus 17:5–8.** God miraculously provides water from a rock to quench the thirst of the Israelites. He has the power to care for His people even in challenging circumstances.

27. **Amalek Defeated – Exodus 17:9–13.** The Amalekites are defeated by the Israelites under Joshua's leadership, showcasing God's support and intervention in battle as Moses holds up his hands in prayer.

28. **Fire Consumed Aaron's Sacrifice – Leviticus 9:24.** Fire from God's presence consumes Aaron's sacrifice, confirming that God approves and accepts the offering. This highlights the importance of proper worship in Israelite religious practices.

29. **Water From the Rock at Meribah – Numbers 20:8–11.** God performs a miracle by instructing Moses to strike a rock, from which water gushes forth to quench the thirst of the Israelites in the desert, demonstrating His ability to provide and care for His people.

30. **Brazen Serpent Healed Those Bitten by Fiery Serpents — Numbers 21:9.** God instructs Moses to craft a bronze serpent, which when looked upon by those bitten by fiery serpents, brings healing and salvation. This miracle reveals the power of faith and God's ability to provide redemption and deliverance from affliction.

31. **Jordan River Supernaturally Divides — Joshua 3:14–17.** God miraculously divides the waters of the Jordan River, allowing the Israelites to cross on dry land into the Promised Land. His power and faithfulness are certain in fulfilling His promises to His people.

32. **The Fall of Jericho — Joshua 6:6–20.** The walls protecting Jericho collapse after the Israelites march around the city for seven days with a final shout of praise, as instructed by God. This intervention by God is part of the fulfillment of His promise to give them the land of Canaan.

33. **Dew on Gideon's Fleece — Judges 6:37–40.** Gideon asks God for a sign using a fleece, requesting dew only on the fleece while the ground remains dry, and then vice versa. God grants Gideon's request, confirming His presence with Gideon as he prepares to lead Israel against the Midianites.

34. **Sun and Moon Stood Still — Joshua 10:12–14.** Joshua prays that the sun and moon stand still, prolonging daylight to secure a victory in battle against the Amorites. This miraculous event reveals God's power and intervention on behalf of His people.

35. **Angel in Flame — Judges 13:20.** An angel appears to Manoah and his wife in a flame on the altar of their offering. This miracle confirmed to them the divine nature of their encounter and the birth of their son Samson.

36. **Thirty Philistines Killed by Samson — Judges 14:19.** Samson kills thirty Philistines in a display of strength and divine assistance, highlighting God's empowerment of Samson and His role in delivering the Israelites from their enemies.

37. **Water from a Hollow Place — Judges 15:19.** God miraculously provides water from a hollow place in the ground at Lehi to quench Samson's thirst after a great victory over the Philistines.

38. **Dagon's Temple Pulled Down by Samson — Judges 16:29–30.** Samson, with supernatural strength, pushes down the pillars of Dagon's temple, causing it to collapse and resulting in the destruction of many Philistine leaders, along with himself. This was God's judgment on idolatry.

39. **Dagon Falls Before the Ark — 1 Samuel 5:1–12.** The idol Dagon falls before the ark of the covenant, first losing its place and then breaking apart, demonstrating God's supremacy over false gods and His power to humble the idols of the nations before His presence.

40. **Samuel Calls Rain at Harvest — 1 Samuel 12:18.** Samuel calls for rain during the wheat harvest as a sign of God's approval and authority, because He wanted to show His ability to control nature and provide for His people's needs in response to repentance and prayer.

41. **Jeroboam's Hand Withered and Healed — 1 Kings 13:4–6.** Jeroboam's hand withers after he orders a man of God to be seized, but it is healed through the prophet's intercession, illustrating God's power to bring judgment and restoration, as well as the authority of His chosen messengers.

42. **The Altar at Bethel Splits — 1 Kings 13:5.** The altar at Bethel splits apart miraculously, signifying God's disapproval of Jeroboam's idolatrous practices and reaffirming the authority of His chosen prophet who had come to deliver His message.

43. **Drought Ordered by Elijah — 1 Kings 17:1; James 5:17.** Elijah prays for a drought upon the land as a judgment from God. This event highlights Elijah's role as a prophet of God who wielded the power of prayer and demonstrated God's sovereignty over nature.

44. **Elijah Fed by Ravens – 1 Kings 17:4-6.** During a time of drought, God miraculously provides for the prophet Elijah by sending ravens to bring him food. God uses unconventional means to care for His faithful servants even in challenging circumstances.

45. **Widow's Oil and Meal Supernaturally Increases – 1 Kings 17:12-17.** God miraculously multiplies the widow's oil and meal, providing an ongoing supply during the drought. God reveals His faithfulness and provision to those who trust in Him in scarce times.

46. **Widow's Son Raised from the Dead – 1 Kings 17:17-23.** Elijah prays, and God shows His power over life and death and His compassion towards those who put their trust in Him and raises the widow's son from the dead.

47. **Elijah's Sacrifice Consumed by Fire – 1 Kings 18:38.** Fire from Heaven falls on Elijah's sacrifice and consumes it, confirming God's presence and power. This miracle signifies God's acceptance of Elijah's offering and leads to the people's acknowledgment of God's supremacy.

48. **Rain Comes in Answer to Prayer – 1 Kings 18:41-45.** Elijah prays, and it begins to rain, ending the drought. God's control over nature and His faithfulness in fulfilling His promises to those who seek Him in prayer is unmistakable.

49. **The Jordan Divided by Elijah's Mantle – 2 Kings 2:8.** Elijah divides the waters of the Jordan River by striking it with his cloak, demonstrating God's power working through His prophet and symbolizing the passing of leadership to Elisha as Elijah's successor.

50. **Elijah Translated to Heaven in a Fiery Chariot – 2 Kings 2:11.** Elijah is taken up to Heaven in a chariot of fire, revealing God's extraordinary intervention and power over life and death, while also marking the conclusion of Elijah's earthly ministry and the transfer of a double portion of his spirit to Elisha.

51. **The Waters of Jericho Healed – 2 Kings 2:20-22.** Elisha heals a spring that provides water for Jericho. He throws salt into the water and declares it is pure. This was God's power to restore and purify, as well as affirm Elisha's new authority as a prophet.

52. **Forty-two Mockers of Elisha Mauled by Bears – 2 Kings 2:24.** Elisha cursed the men that mocked him, and then they are mauled by bears, which shows God's defense of His prophet's honor.

53. **Elisha Prophesies and Water Fills the Land – 2 Kings 3:16-20.** As the musician played, Elisha prophesied that an abundance of water would come. The next day, water fills the land.

54. **Widow's Oil Multiplies – 2 Kings 4:1-7.** This event highlights God's faithfulness to His promises and His ability to turn scarcity into abundance. It also emphasizes the importance of faith and obedience, as the widow followed the prophet Elisha's instructions and experienced a miraculous provision of oil that exceeded her expectations.

55. **Shunammite's Son Raised From the Dead – 2 Kings 4:19-37.** This is a powerful miracle of God's ability to restore life. It demonstrates God's compassion for a grieving mother and His power over death itself. It also serves as a reminder of the faithfulness of the prophet Elisha and the faith of the Shunammite woman, demonstrating the miraculous intervention of God in response to sincere prayer and trust.

56. **Elisha Feeds a Hundred Men with 20 Loaves – 2 Kings 4:42-44.** This is a unique miracle that demonstrates God's abundant provision and multiplication of resources.

57. **Naaman Cured of Leprosy – 2 Kings 5:10-14.** Naaman, a commander suffering from leprosy, is miraculously cured after following Elisha's instructions to wash in the Jordan River seven times, demonstrating God's power to heal to all who humbly seek Him.

58. **Syrian Army Captured – 2 Kings 6:18–20.** Elisha prays and the Syrian army is temporarily blinded, allowing the Israelites to lead them into their own camp to capture them.

59. **Dead Man Comes Back to Life When He Touches Elisha's Bones – 2 Kings 13:21.** A dead man is thrown into an open grave and his body touches the bones of Elisha, causing him to come back to life. This is a demonstration of God's miraculous power and the anointing of His servants even after their passing and Elisha's final double portion miracle.

60. **185,000 Soldiers Struck Down by an Angel – 2 Kings 19:35.** This happened in the context of a crisis faced by the kingdom of Judah. The Assyrian army, led by King Sennacherib, had besieged Jerusalem and threatened to conquer it. This divine intervention was necessary to deliver Judah from imminent destruction and demonstrate God's power and faithfulness in protecting His chosen people.

61. **Hezekiah is Healed of a Life-Threatening Boil – 2 Kings 20:1–7.** King Hezekiah has a life-threatening boil and is told he will die. He cries out to God in prayer and God heals him and adds fifteen more years to his life. This demonstrates God's power to heal and His responsiveness to sincere prayer.

62. **Shadow on Sundial Moves Backward – 2 Kings 20:11.** King Hezekiah asks for a miraculous sign to guarantee his healing will come. He requests the sundial shadow move backward ten degrees.

63. **Uzziah is Afflicted with Leprosy – 2 Chronicles 26:16–21.** Leprosy appears on King Uzziah's forehead as a divine punishment for his pride and disobedience to burn incense in the temple. It serves as God's justice and the consequences of arrogance and straying from His commands.

64. **Three Men Delivered from a Fiery Furnace – Daniel 3:19–27.** Shadrach, Meshach, and Abednego are delivered from a very hot furnace by God's miraculous intervention, keeping them from being burned or even smelling like smoke. This shows God's power to protect His faithful followers.

65. **Daniel Delivered From a Lion's Den – Daniel 6:16–23.** Due to Daniel's unwavering faithfulness to God and his commitment to prayer, even though a decree forbade praying to any deity besides King Darius, he was cast into the lion's den. Nevertheless, God supernaturally closed the mouths of the lions, ensuring Daniel's protection throughout the night.

66. **Jonah Preserved Inside a Fish for Three Days – Jonah 2:1–10.** This miracle occurred as a result of Jonah's disobedience and attempt to flee from God's command to preach to the people of Nineveh. After being swallowed by the fish, Jonah prayed for deliverance and acknowledged God's sovereignty, leading to his repentance and renewed commitment to fulfill God's will.

New Testament Miracles

1. **Jesus Turns Water to Wine – John 2:1–11.** Jesus performs His first miracle by turning water into wine at a wedding in Cana, revealing His spiritual power and the beginning His ministry.

2. **Nobleman's Son Healed in Cana – John 4:46–54.** Jesus heals the nobleman's son in Cana from a distance with just His word, emphasizing faith as a key element for receiving a miraculous healing. It shows His compassion leading to the nobleman and his household believing in Jesus.

3. **Demoniac in Synagogue Healed – Mark 1:23-26.** Jesus healed a demon-possessed man in a Capernaum synagogue, demonstrating His power over evil spirits and His ability to bring spiritual and physical healing. This miraculous act amazed the witnesses and revealed Jesus' authority over the spirit world.

4. **The Miraculous Catch of Fish – Luke 5:1–11.** Jesus miraculously fills the nets of Peter, James, and John after a night of unsuccessful fishing, showcasing Jesus' power over nature by filling the nets with an abundance of fish but also serves as a call to discipleship for Peter, James, and John.

5. **Leper Cleansed in Capernaum – Matthew 8:1–4.** Jesus cleanses a leper because of His compassion and power to heal even the most ostracized and marginalized individuals. The miracle led to the leper's restoration to the community.

6. **Paralytic Healed in Capernaum – Matthew 9:1–8.** Jesus heals a paralytic, revealing His authority to forgive sins and perform physical healing, which resulted in the crowd glorifying God.

7. **Man Healed in Jerusalem – John 5:1–9.** Jesus heals a man who had been disabled for thirty-eight years at the pool of Bethesda in Jerusalem, showing all that were present His compassion and ability to bring about miraculous healing.

8. **Withered Hand Restored in Galilee – Matthew 12:10–13.** Jesus restores a man's withered hand, indicating His authority to heal and willingness to restore wholeness to those in need, even in the face of opposition from religious leaders.

9. **A Widow's Son Raised from the Dead – Luke 7:11–17.** Jesus raises a widow's son from the dead, showcasing His power over death and His compassion for those who are grieving, leading to awe and praise from the crowd as they recognize the authority of Jesus as a prophet.

10. **Demoniac Healed in Galilee – Matthew 12:22–23.** Jesus heals a demoniac, demonstrating His authority over evil spirits and His power to bring about spiritual and physical healing, leading to wonder and amazement among the people.

11. **Storm on the Sea of Galilee Stilled – Matthew 8:23–27.** Jesus and His disciples are on a boat when a great storm arises on the Sea of Galilee. The disciples are afraid, but Jesus rebukes the winds and the sea, and there is a great calm. This miracle shows Jesus' power over nature and teaches His disciples about faith and trust in Him, even in the midst of trials.

12. **Demons Went into a Herd of Pigs – Matthew 8:28–34.** Jesus encounters two demon-possessed men in the Gadarene region. He commands the demons to leave the men, who then enter a herd of pigs, causing them to run into the sea and drown. Jesus has authority over demons and devils.

13. **Jairus' Daughter Raised from the Dead – Matthew 9:23–25.** Jairus, a synagogue leader, asks Jesus to heal his daughter who has died. Jesus goes to Jairus'

house, takes her by the hand, and she gets up. This miracle increases Jesus' fame in the region.

14. **Woman with Issue of Blood Healed — Matthew 9:20–22.** A woman suffering from a hemorrhage for twelve years believes if she can touch His cloak she would be healed. When she does, she is instantly healed. Jesus commends her for her faith.

15. **Two Blind Men Healed — Matthew 9:27–31.** Two men who were blind approach Jesus, asking for mercy. Jesus touches their eyes, and they are healed, receiving their sight.

16. **Mute Spirit Cast Out — Matthew 9:32–33.** Jesus casts out a spirit that prevents a man from speaking in Capernaum, enabling him to talk. This miracle displays Jesus' authority over spiritual oppression and His power to restore wholeness to those who are afflicted.

17. **Five Thousand Fed Supernaturally — Matthew 14:15–21.** Jesus has compassion on the crowd and miraculously feeds five thousand people with only five loaves of bread and two fish.

18. **Jesus Walks on the Sea of Galilee — Matthew 14:25–33.** During a storm, Jesus walks on the water to meet His disciples, who are in their boat. Jesus had power over air, land, and sea. Inspired by faith, Peter briefly walks on water before faltering.

19. **A Canaanite Daughter Healed of a Demon — Matthew 15:21–28.** A Canaanite woman pleads with Jesus to heal her demon-possessed daughter. Jesus initially tests her faith, but upon seeing her persistent and genuine belief, He heals her.

20. **Four Thousand Supernaturally Fed — Matthew 15:32–39.** Jesus supernaturally feeds a crowd of four thousand people with just seven loaves of bread and a few fish, revealing His miraculous power and abundant provision for those in need.

21. **Transfiguration of Christ and Moses and Elijah Appear — Matthew 17:1–7.** Jesus is transfigured before His disciples, and Moses and Elijah appear with Him. This event reveals Jesus' divine glory, confirms His authority, and represents the fulfillment of the Law and the Prophets in Him.

22. **Tax Money Appears in Fish's Mouth — Matthew 17:24–27.** Jesus instructs Peter to find money in a fish's mouth to pay the temple tax, which says He can supernaturally provide and give wisdom in meeting financial obligations.

23. **Jesus Casts Out an Unclean Spirit — Mark 1:23–28.** Jesus casts out an unclean spirit from a man in the synagogue. This confirms His authority over evil forces and His divine identity as the Son of God.

24. **Deaf and Dumb Man healed — Mark 7:31–37.** Jesus heals a man who cannot speak or hear, confirming His authority over physical ailments and His compassion for those in need. This miracle emphasizes Jesus' ability to bring wholeness to individuals.

25. **Blind Man Healed — Mark 8:22–26.** Jesus heals a blind man in two stages, first partially restoring his sight and then He heals him fully. This indicates there can be a gradual approach to healing.

26. **A Demon Cast Out of Boy with Seizures — Mark 9:14–29.** Jesus casts out a demon from a boy who has epileptic fits. Jesus has the power to bring deliverance and healing to those in distress. This event shows the importance of faith and prayer in seeking God's intervention in difficult situations.

27. **Ten Lepers Cleansed — Luke 17:11–19.** Ten lepers come to Jesus and He heals them. But only one returns to say thank you. This miracle underscores the significance of gratitude and the importance of acknowledging God's mercy and blessings in our lives.

28. **Man Born Blind Healed — John 9:1–7.** Jesus heals a man who was blind from birth by making mud with His saliva, applying it to the man's eyes, and instructing him to wash in the pool of Siloam. This miracle demonstrates Jesus' power to bring physical healing and the importance of obedience.

29. **Lazarus Raised from Dead — John 11:38–44.** After being dead for three days, Jesus commands Lazarus to come out of the tomb, and he walks out covered in grave clothes. This shows Jesus' authority over death and points to His own resurrection. This miracle also indicates Jesus' deep care for His friends, revealing He is the giver of life.

30. **Woman with Infirmity Cured — Luke 13:11–17.** Jesus heals a woman who had been crippled for eighteen years. This miracle underscores Jesus' desire to bring healing and restoration to those who suffer, showing His love and care for individuals.

31. **Man with Dropsy is Healed — Luke 14:1–6.** Jesus heals a man who had extreme swelling because of an accumulation of fluids. Jesus showed compassion and the ability to restore health, even on the Sabbath.

32. **A Blind Man Healed on the Jericho Road — Luke 18:35–43.** The blind man's persistent faith in calling out to Jesus despite obstacles and discouragement showed the importance of faith in receiving God's blessings. It teaches us the value of perseverance and trust in God's ability to intervene in our lives.

33. **Fig Tree Cursed and Withers — Mark 11:12–14, 20.** Jesus curses a fig tree because it doesn't bear fruit, causing it to wither. The event serves as a symbolic act of the consequences of spiritual barrenness and hypocrisy and highlights Jesus' authority and power to bring about visible signs in nature that reflect deeper spiritual truths.

34. **Malchus' Ear Healed — Luke 22:50–51.** Jesus heals the ear of a servant of the high priest, who was injured during His arrest. This act is indicative of Jesus' compassion and non-violent nature, even in the face of hostility and conflict.

35. **Jesus Heals an Invalid Man at the Pool of Bethesda — John 5:1–9.** A man who had been lying by the Bethesda Pool for many years, unable to enter the water when it was stirred for healing, is seen by Jesus. Jesus has compassion on him and instantly heals him.

36. **Second Draught of Fish — John 21:1–14.** Jesus performs a second miraculous catch of fish for His disciples. This miracle revealed His ability to provide, His authority over nature, and reaffirmed His call for them to be fishers of men. There is an abundance of blessings and opportunities that come from following Jesus obediently.

37. **Resurrection of Christ — Luke 24:6.** The angels declare to the women at the tomb, "He is not here; He has risen!" This event marks the resurrection of Jesus Christ, which is the central event of our faith. The resurrection of Jesus brings victory over sin and death and offers hope and eternal life to all Believers.

38. **Christ Appears to Mary Magdalene — Mark 16:9.** Jesus affirms the reality of His resurrection by appearing to Mary Magdalene after His death. In doing so, Jesus shows His personal care for His followers.

39. **Christ Appears to Other Women — Matthew 28:9.** After His resurrection, Jesus appears to other women besides Mary Magdalene, fulfilling His promise of resurrection, bringing hope and joy to His followers.

40. **Christ Appears to Two Disciples — Luke 24:15–31.** Jesus appears to two disciples on the road to Emmaus. They don't recognize Him until He breaks bread. Jesus' presence is with His followers even in moments of doubt and confusion.

41. **Christ Appears to Peter — 1 Corinthians 15:5.** Jesus appears to Peter after His resurrection, personally confirming to him His victory over death. This is the extending of grace, forgiveness, and restoration to Peter despite his earlier denial.

42. **Christ Appears to Ten Disciples — John 20:19–24.** Jesus appears to ten of His disciples (Thomas being absent), showing them His resurrected body and solidifying their faith in His resurrection and commissioning them for their mission to spread the Good News.

43. **Christ Appears to Eleven Disciples – John 20:26–28.** Jesus appears to the eleven disciples, including Thomas, showing them His resurrected body and inviting Thomas to touch His wounds. Thomas affirms his faith in Jesus as Lord and God, reinforcing the reality of Jesus' resurrection and the importance of faith in Him.

44. **Christ Appears to Seven Disciples Fishing – John 21:1–24.** While seven of Jesus disciples were fishing, Jesus appears to them. He wanted to show them His continued presence and care for His followers even after His resurrection. This miracle reaffirms His commission to His disciples, symbolized by the miraculous catch of fish and the reinstatement of Peter after his denial.

45. **Christ Appears to James – 1 Corinthians 15:7.** It is mentioned that Jesus appeared to James after His resurrection, which highlights the personal encounters Jesus had with His disciples to confirm His victory over death and His resurrection. Jesus wanted to strengthen the faith of His followers and commission them for ministry.

46. **Christ Appears to Eleven Disciples on Day of Ascension – Acts 1:2–9.** Jesus appears to the eleven disciples when He was to ascend into heaven and commissions them to continue His work of spreading the Gospel to all nations. This event marks the culmination of Jesus' earthly ministry and the beginning of the disciples' mission empowered by the Holy Spirit.

47. **Outpouring of the Holy Spirit – Acts 2:1–14.** The Holy Spirit descends on the disciples on the day of Pentecost, empowering them with supernatural gifts and enabling them to speak in different languages. This event marks the birth of the early church and the fulfillment of Jesus' promise to send the Holy Spirit, equipping Believers for ministry and spreading the message of salvation to people of all nations.

48. **Peter Heals Lame Man – Acts 3:6–7.** Peter heals a lame man by commanding him to walk "in the name of Jesus Christ of Nazareth." This miracle demonstrates the authority and power of Jesus' name and the transformative impact of faith in Him. It also serves as a testimony to the reality of Jesus' resurrection and the continued ministry of healing through His followers.

49. **Peter Heals Many Sick People – Acts 5:15–16.** Peter performs miraculous healings on many sick people, showcasing the power of God's Spirit working through the apostles and affirming the authenticity of their ministry.

50. **Apostles Freed from Prison by an Angel – Acts 5:19.** This miraculous escape of several apostles from prison illustrates God's intervention in the lives of His faithful servants, even in the face of severe persecution and difficult circumstances.

51. **Stephen Performs Great Miracles – Acts 6:8.** Stephen did many mighty miracles because of the supernatural power of God at work in his ministry. The miracles confirmed he was a faithful servant and witness for Jesus Christ.

52. **Philip Casts Out Unclean Spirits – Acts 8:6–7.** Unclean spirits are cast out of people by Peter, and he heals many who were lame and paralyzed. The authority and power of the Holy Spirit worked through him to bring about miraculous healings and deliverance.

53. **Paul's Eyesight is Restored – Acts 9:17–18.** Paul was able to see again after Ananias prays for him, confirming his spiritual transformation and commissioning as an apostle by God. This miracle also underscores God's sovereignty in orchestrating significant events in Paul's life.

54. **Paralyzed Aeneas is Healed by Peter – Acts 9:33–35.** This miracle serves to authenticate Peter's ministry as an apostle and reinforces the message of Jesus' ability to bring about physical healing. It also brings glory to God and strengthens the faith of those who witness miraculous healing.

55. **Dorcas Raised from the Dead – Acts 9:40.** After Dorcas' death, Peter kneels, prays, and commands her

to get up. She sits up, and Peter presents her alive to those gathered. The power of God works through Peter to perform miracles, bringing about life where there was death and strengthening the faith of Believers in the resurrection power of Jesus Christ.

56. **Cornelius' Vision – Acts 10:3–4, 30–32.** Cornelius has a vision in which an angel instructs him to send for Peter. It marks the beginning of Gentile inclusion in the early Christian community and underscores God's desire for all people to receive the message of salvation through Jesus Christ, regardless of their background.

57. **Peter Freed From Prison by an Angel – Acts 12:7–11.** An angel of the Lord frees Peter from prison, while the Believers are praying for him. God has the power to deliver His servants from adversity, injustice, and persecution. This miraculous event also emphasizes the importance of prayer and the divine protection that accompanies those who are faithful to God's purposes.

58. **Elymas, the Sorcerer, is Blinded – Acts 13:11.** Elymas, a deceitful sorcerer, is blinded by Paul, showing God's power and judgment upon those who oppose the truth and resist the work of God. It also caused government leaders to believe in Jesus.

59. **Lame Man Cured by Paul – Acts 14:10.** Paul demonstrated the power and authority of God working through him by healing a man who couldn't walk. God, being compassionate, can bring about physical healing in response to faith.

60. **Young Woman Delivered of Evil Spirit – Acts 16:16–18.** An evil spirit in a slave girl gave her the ability to tell people's fortunes, bringing her owners much money. Paul commands the spirit to leave her, and it does. This event emphasizes the spiritual battle present in Christian ministry and underscores the importance of discernment and prayer in confronting spiritual oppression.

61. **Earthquake Releases Paul and Silas from Prison – Acts 16:25–26.** The earthquake that released Paul and Silas from prison was the result of their faithful worship to God despite being imprisoned unjustly. The miracles also caused the jailer and his family to believe in Jesus.

62. **Twelve Men Receive the Gift of Tongues and Prophesied – Acts 19:6.** Paul lays hands on twelve men and they receive the Holy Spirit, the gift of tongues, and begin to prophesy. This miracle demonstrates the supernatural empowerment and manifestation of spiritual gifts among Believers.

63. **Special Miracles by Paul – Acts 19:11–12.** There were many other unique miracles that Paul performed, including handkerchiefs or aprons that touched his body being taken to the sick. Their diseases were cured, and evil spirits left them. These miracles reveal the extraordinary power of God working through Paul, confirming his apostolic authority, and emphasizing the effectiveness of faith and the anointing of the Holy Spirit in bringing about healing and deliverance.

64. **Eutychus Died and Brought Back to Life – Acts 20:9–11.** Eutychus falls from a window and dies but is brought back to life by Paul. Once again, the power of God works through Paul to perform a resurrection, reaffirming God's compassion and ability to bring life even in the face of death.

65. **Publius' Father is Healed – Acts 28:8.** Paul heals Publius' father on the island of Malta, confirming God's power to bring about miraculous healing through His chosen apostles to those of other cultures.

66. **Innumerable Miracles of Christ Witnessed by the Disciples – John 20:30; cf. Acts 10:38–39.** The Bible mentions that there were many other signs and miracles performed by Jesus in the presence of His disciples, which were not specifically recorded. Acts 10:38–39 says Jesus went about doing good and healing all who were oppressed by the devil. There was an abundance of miraculous works that Jesus performed during His ministry, indicating that His Father's power and favor were with Him, as well as the compassion He had for those in need.

When you pray, believe that you will receive it, and you will have it. Watch His miracles come to pass.

- JOEL

About Joel Osteen

Joel Osteen is senior pastor of Lakewood Church in Houston, Texas — a vibrant and diverse church that Forbes has called the largest and fastest growing congregation in America. As a #1 *New York Times* bestselling author, Joel shares a positive message of hope and encouragement that extends all around the world. Joel's television broadcast is the most watched inspirational program in America.

Discover more at **JoelOsteen.com.**

Stay encouraged *and* inspired all through the week.

Download the Joel Osteen Daily Podcast *and* **subscribe now** *on* **YouTube to get the latest videos.**

For a full listing, visit **JoelOsteen.com/How-To-Watch**.

Apple Podcasts

Stay connected, *be* blessed.

Get more from Joel & Victoria Osteen

It's time to step into the life of victory and favor that God has planned for you! Featuring new messages from Joel & Victoria Osteen, their free daily devotional, and inspiring articles, hope is always at your fingertips with the free Joel Osteen app and online at JoelOsteen.com.

Get the app and visit us today at JoelOsteen.com.

CONNECT WITH US